More Valley
Animals
2020

More Valley Animals 2020

Written by
Brooks Firestone

•

Illustrated by
Alasdair Hilleary

To my wife, Kate Firestone,
who loves and supports Valley animals
and her husband.

To friends, neighbors, and animals in the Valley
that have provided a rare and wonderful home for our family.

Firestone, Brooks.
More Valley Animals 2020: True stories about the animals and people of California's Santa
Ynez Valley, 2nd Edition / by Brooks Firestone.
ISBN 978-1-735-8770-1-3 (Paperback)
1. Animals—California—Santa Ynez River Valley—Anecdotes.
2. Domestic animals—California—Santa Ynez River Valley—Anecdotes.
3. Santa Ynez River Valley (Calif.)—Anecdotes. 1. Title.

LIBRARY OF CONGRESS CATALOGUING-IN-PUBLICATION DATA

ISBN 978-1-735-8770-1-3 (Paperback)

Book Designed by:
Two Trumpets Communications
4939 Carpinteria Ave., Carpinteria, CA 93013
(805) 453-4878 • www.2trumpets.com
&
Published and Distributed by:
Polyverse Publications
1035 Palmetto Way, Unit J., Carpinteria, CA 93013
805-294-2741 • www.polyversepublications.com

Printed in the United States of America
10 9 8 7 6 5 4 3 2

CONTENTS

Part I: Wild Things

Part II: Commercial Enterprise

Part III: Ranch Work

Part IV: Domestic Partners

Part V: Country Moments

Introduction

Ten years ago, I sat down to write a book of animal stories that I had collected over my years of living in the Santa Ynez Valley. My purpose was to illustrate something of our life and culture, as well as the unique way of being and the friendly, "down to earth," generous outlook that is found here. There was also a desire to help perpetuate our Valley lifestyle by describing the interaction with animals that defines our nature.

Now, ten years later, I have searched anew for animal interactions that represent who we are, and attempted to write those stories. Of course, there are more of us, the roads are more crowded, and the press of urbanization has weighed heavily on our rural flavor. But the animals are by and large the same, and the essential culture and outlook of Valley people has not changed all that much. There is less farming and ranching and more tourism and commuting, but otherwise, the Valley is the Valley.

By the way, once again, all the episodes are true and factually accurate with only small details and names left out because of legal complications or shy individuals.

In the first book, published in 2010, I wrote from the stories collected over twenty-five years. Now, with the second volume, and with less time for story collection, I had some difficulty finding enough material. There are fewer ranching stories because there are fewer ranchers, but our household animals still live with and off us, and although the wilder animals that haunt our hills have retreated somewhat from the expanded people activity, they still interact on the border between urban and open.

That basic Valley relationship with our animal friends has maintained in our culture and way of life and, hopefully, will always maintain. Best of all, it is a joy to tell these stories, rejoicing that people and creatures continue to get along together in a way that defines our Valley.

My fondest dream and ambition is to be around to write more animal stories ten years from now, and that those stories will still define who we are. All of us in the Valley can only hope the essential way of living with each other and with animals will not change too much in the next ten years. Our Valley animals would probably be happy with that also.

I am grateful that my friend Alasdair Hilleary agreed to illustrate the book once again. His Scottish humor and sensitivity to animals adds immensely to the stories. My wife, Kate, has been a great help in reading my drafts and encouraging my efforts. Melinda Masson has been a genius editor in sorting out my grammar, spelling, and awkward turns of phrase. I am grateful to Lea Boyd, publishing agent, and Louis Force Torres for publishing details and promotional help. Most of all, I am grateful to all those who have related their stories, which are the substance of the book. Thank you all for everything that has made this book possible.

Authors usually dedicate their work, and my dedication is simply to the Valley. Kate and I found this happy place in 1972, and it will be home forever. Thank you, Valley!

About the Author

Brooks and Kate Firestone, married in 1958, moved to the Santa Ynez Valley in 1972 to found the Firestone Vineyard Winery. They now include a family of four children, fourteen grandchildren, and four great-grandchildren.

Brooks was raised in Los Angeles and, after graduating from Columbia College and a two-year draft in the U.S. Army, worked for twelve years in the Firestone Tire and Rubber Company founded by his grandfather. In addition to the winery career, the family lived on a working cattle ranch for twenty-five years in the Valley, and Brooks served in the California Assembly and as Santa Barbara County Third District Supervisor.

Brooks has an abiding appreciation for the life of the Santa Ynez Valley, and the people and animals who live here. This enthusiasm brought him in 2010 and 2020 to write two books of stories that illustrate the life and culture of his home country.

About the Illustrator

Alasdair Hilleary is a sixty-five-year-old cartoonist (signee "Loon") living in the Highlands of Scotland. Having been first brought to the Santa Ynez Valley on their honeymoon by his late wife Fiona in 1984 (an old and good friend of the author's family), they stayed for nine happy months painting his cartoons and working their passage. He is now a regular visitor to the Valley, as a recent member of Los Rancheros Visitadores, and has many friends in the Valley.

He began his cartooning career with a London "sellout" exhibition in 1978, having first served a four-year commission in the Scots Guards; he has exhibited in many places around the world since then, and his work can be found in many private collections including several with the royal family.

His work can be found online (www.looncartoons.co.uk), in Dracula's Club, St. Moritz, in The Hong Kong Club, and in many private houses around the world. Brought up in Scotland, his father is a serial entrepreneur-cum-Special Forces veteran, and his late mother a double Olympic champion skier. There was always an emphasis on enjoying every aspect of life to the best of one's ability, to laugh, to love, and to be kind (some of which is reflected in his work)!

Part One

WILD THINGS

Cool Cats

Not long ago, a couple of local characters, man and animal, had a quiet meeting that serves as a portrait depicting the relationship of Valley animals and people, the old and the new, the past and the future. This chance face-off might serve to illustrate the greater phenomena of our country life.

Jim Pugh moved to the Valley in the early 2000s, intending a country landing space for his family after a stellar jazz piano career. The Pugh family took to the Valley as a welcome change from the city and jazz travel life. His career included Grammy Awards, platinum and gold records, ten years with singer Etta James, and twenty-five years playing backup for singer Robert Cray on road tours. His six-foot-five frame, friendly and modest demeanor, dry sense of humor, and maturity describe something far beyond the jazz world, and someone who would fit in well, Valley-wise.

Jim is the founder of the Little Village Foundation, which provides encouragement, venues, and inspiration for young musicians from all backgrounds. The organization is a serious contribution to the California music scene and a giveback that could only be inspired by the talent and good intentions of a Jim Pugh. He also sings occasionally in the St. Mark's choir because he likes doing it and is a good singer as well as everything else. But he is still a city kid.

When he moved to the Valley, he wanted to fit into the life here, and do a country activity by way of something very different from the jazz-roadie life and concert scene. Good fortune led him to Carol "Puck" Erickson—a Valley character, brilliant horticulturist, and founder of the Santa Ynez Valley Botanic Garden. Botanical advisor Eva Powers is the dedicated and able president of the current foundation that maintains the garden park open to the public. Perhaps the 1800s Spanish rancheros and past-century ranchers did not envision the necessity of a park, established in 2006, to promote the natural beauty of the Valley, but our modern Valley people are served very well by this splendid organization.

As mentioned, Jim wanted a Valley activity, and Puck needed volunteer help, so the pianist wound up shoveling and raking mulch to the plant beds, a never-ending job in the garden that even a famous jazz musician could accomplish. The work suited Jim, and he could choose his own hours and often worked on his own. One bright and chilly Valley morning found him by himself happily wheelbarrowing mulch, feeling at peace and at one with the country life.

In the morning quiet, a large cat emerged from under a park bridge and sauntered toward Jim. His instinct was to approach the frowsy cat and make friends. Something in the air caused a pause as the two approached each other. Man and cat stood looking, a few feet apart. The cat was quiet and observant, and Jim was curious, with a little prickle up his spine. It was a good thing that the cat was an old hand and not given to unnecessary confrontation. It was a good thing that Jim was a big man, topped off with a hat and carrying a shovel.

After a silent moment, the big cat quietly turned and padded off back under the bridge. Jim continued shoveling mulch.

A little later, Puck drove in to do her supervisory thing and greeted her shoveling volunteer. Jim told her about the big cat. "That was no cat," she replied. "That was a mountain lion that has been seen around here!"

The meeting contained a significant symbolism. The old and future Valley met and observed each other. A famous jazz musician had found the Valley, moved in, and wanted to do the right thing by the country. A local lion going about traditional country business was curious about the new people. The two got along and parted in peace. That is our Valley.

Fresh Contraband

Fish stories come in many varieties, usually exaggerated and embellished, sometimes startling and true. This is not technically a Valley story, but

Valley characters were involved, and it is a good tale.

The incident is attested to by a local who was in the boat and in on the heist, but is still sufficiently nervous and guilt ridden that he tells the story rarely, and only on condition of complete anonymity. A well-known Santa Barbara character, Silvio Di Loreto, was also a member of the boat party, and he can be identified because, sadly, he is no longer with us, and his statute of limitations is thereby expired.

Years ago, five good friends cast off in a comfortable powerboat from the Santa Barbara Harbor for a sunny day of conviviality, fishing, and scuba diving across the channel near Santa Cruz Island. The air was calm and perfect. Their lunch was delicious, the drinks were cold and mood inducing, the clear water was welcoming, and the conversation flourished. Incidentally, the men dropped their lines and caught a few dinner fish and a few uglies that they tossed back into the sea. The scuba part was refreshing if not productive.

As the afternoon waned, they finally decided to head for home. The friends stored their gear, settled back, and, in no hurry, made their leisurely way to shore. The atmosphere was dozy, but fortunately, one man in the front of the boat was alert, and urgently whispered to the skipper to cut the engine. He did, and the boatload of curiosity drifted toward something large in the water.

We don't think of fish sleeping, but this shiny, languid, basking form appeared to be in a deep slumber, totally unaware of the world, and dead ahead of the quiet boat. The awestruck fishing party silently seized nets, gaffs, and a spear that handily appeared from under the seats, and sprang into an entirely new style of fishing.

The next scene unfolded amid confusion, cage-wrestling mayhem, heroic shouts, and desperate grapplings. Five otherwise father figures were now engaged in deadly combat versus, of all things, a rudely awakened, 125-pound fighting swordfish!

It is rare, but large fish do bask and doze on the ocean surface. This one was obviously dreaming of far-off places, and the surprise was total, but deeply insulting to fish dignity—imagine the swordfish energy that arose! But the fish was speared, gaffed, netted, and beset by five desperate friends, heroically dedicated to landing this trophy. Fortunately, the long swordlike beak did not figure in the struggle. There were cuts and bruises, and later aches and pains, but ultimately the team prevailed, and the prize fish lay gutted and strapped to the stern swim step.

The day rapidly changed to earnest purpose as the engine ran the boat at full speed back toward the harbor. The friends looked at each other and plotted. True, they had experienced an adventure and won a trophy beyond any rock-fishing dreams, but they also had a highly illegal catch, closely controlled and watched by authorities and professional fishermen alike. Severe penalties, possibly even felonies, could enter into their sportfishing scenario with the discovery of this incident. A swordfish is a carefully protected species, and only those with an expensive license can hope to land and register one legally. But the five men also had a rare fish story for trusted friends, as well as the best of all feasts on fresh grilled swordfish.

As indicated, the five were substantial local worthies, not without resources, larceny, and creative law avoidance within their capabilities. Above all, they could not return to the harbor or be spotted by any professional fisherman, Fish and Wildlife official, Harbor official, Coast Guard officer, or other in authority, as that might lead to arrest. They counseled long and hard as they sped home, and came up with a plan.

The now-contraband craft pulled up offshore Goleta Beach, hovering far from prying harbor eyes, just outside the kelp bed in calm water. The conspirators closely eyeballed the beachgoers for sheriff's deputies, or anyone in official capacity. Silvio, the most experienced scuba diver, donned his wetsuit and slipped into the ocean, while the others fastened a short rope around the fish's tail. Silvio hovered in the water, dangling the big fish and hoping for a sharkless day, while the boat sped back to the harbor. The friends casually docked and innocently unloaded picnic and fishing gear as usual, and hastened to their station wagon. They then sped around to the beach to rescue Silvio and their trophy.

At Goleta Beach, they parked and waved their confederate to shore. The beach crowd stared in amazement as a wetsuited figure emerged with a monster fish, complete with frontal spear, from where they had all been recently swimming. Our five ran the fish up to the station wagon where towels and jackets quickly covered the trophy, all except the sword sticking out. The furtive gang jumped in and sped off, Silvio still in his wetsuit, leaving the nonplussed beach crowd wondering whether they might have been swimming in monster-fish-infested waters.

On returning home, our fishermen had a spectacular answer to the age-old question, "Honey, did you catch anything?" Later that evening, family and intimate friends shared the fish barbecue of their lives amid the heroic tale, which has remained top secret among boat people. The friends were sufficiently spooked not to mount the 125-pound specimen or boast for many years, and the story is only now emerging.

Black Cat

One of the perennial Valley animal mysteries was reignited in the summer of 2018 when at the Fess Parker Winery area, off the Foxen Canyon Road, a vineyard worker captured a video of a large black cat moving between sidehill oak trees. The scene was foreign and spooky, and the Valley Black Cat Saga continued with new evidence.

Close analysis and a consultation with the California Department of Fish and Wildlife could only conclude that this was a black mountain lion, otherwise known as a black panther. Conversations with ranchers and old-timers have confirmed these fleeting glimpses of "black cats" in our hills that attest to their existence, if not the specifics of where they may have originated. Sightings have haunted the Valley for years.

Black panthers exist around the world, mostly as Asian leopards who for some reason have a large dose of melanin, an ingredient for dark skin coat. They faintly retain their spots, obscured beneath a dark coat, and this mysterious and sinister coloring makes the cats highly prized by zoos. Black-looking jaguars are seen in northern Mexico, but never this far north of the border. The vineyard worker's video was the first concrete proof of the rumors of Valley mystery sightings.

Two zoo-type operations are known to have existed in modern Valley times. Andersen's Animal Park was owned by famed movie animal trainers Pat and Ted Derby in the late 1960s. In addition to advocating for the ethical treatment of captive animals, the two made an effort to lure Highway 101 travelers stopping for the famous pea soup to buy a ticket and see their impressive menagerie that included at least one of the Collie dogs who starred as the movie hero Lassie. When the enterprise failed, Valley talk among old-timers was that some of the animals were given their freedom. Among these animals, a black jaguar, imported from Mexico, may have been let loose to hunt prey and seek romance in our Valley foothills, and thereby established the genetics for whatever big cat was caught on the winery worker's film.

Many Valley residents were employees at Michael Jackson's Neverland Ranch from 1988 to its sale in 2008. All the employees were subject to nondisclosure agreements and threats of severe penalties and lawsuits if anything was spoken about the ranch or, of course, Michael Jackson. For this reason, not much is known about the operation of the ranch or the zoo that was a central feature.

But rumor in the Valley maintains that an amazing collection of animals was cared for on the ranch, and the Neverland menagerie included at least one "black panther." No wild-animal operation is perfect, and one managed by employees more familiar with domestic livestock might be assumed to have more incidents than a professional zoo. Escapes did occur, and although there is absolutely no factual confirmation of this theory, a wily Michael Jackson cat, yearning for distant hills, may very much be the family ancestor of our mysterious black cat found in the same area in 2018.

The only other natural explanation for our sightings might be a distant and heroic migration from the hills of Mexico, where black jaguars have been known to roam. These undocumented visitors would adapt very happily to our Valley.

Mountain lions abound in our Valley hills, and the nocturnal cats are rarely seen because they are even more shy of people than people are of them. But the rare and exciting view of a large black cat may well become a Valley phenomenon, even if the origin of the animals will probably never be known. The Valley Black Cat Saga is, doubtless, to be continued.

· 🄵 ·

Opossum Therapy

One early morning on a chilly winter's day in the Valley, a Los Angeles tourist couple emerged from a local hostelry to find their Volkswagen would not start. On lifting the hood, they discovered that the reason was a mother opossum with ten babies housed in the engine area. The opossum family was uninjured, but not inclined to leave, having found a warm refuge in the cold night. The driver was not about to reach in to free the hitchhikers, but could not move on with them nested in the engine compartment. Fortunately, the person on duty at the hotel desk knew of the "Possum Lady," and made a call.

Dawn Summerlin, a retired nurse living in Buellton, has devoted her medical and rescue skills to a career in saving injured or stranded opossums in our Valley. She first came upon the species when volunteering with the Santa Barbara Wildlife Care Network, shortly after moving to the Valley in the mid-1990s. When one day a mother opossum with five young was dropped off at the Goleta shelter, she asked to take them home for care and release. She did not figure on falling in love with these animals, but that just happened, and she has been nursing opossums-in-distress ever since.

Opossums are nocturnal, marsupial land mammals with a prehensile tail, who live two to three years, grow twenty-four to thirty-four inches long, and weigh four to twelve pounds. Nocturnal means they hide out during the day and travel by night because they do not see well but have excellent hearing and scenting. Marsupial means they have a pouch for their young (and are related to kangaroos); in fact, opossums are the only such animal in North America. The prehensile tail allows them to maneuver and sometimes hang by the long and strong appendage. Their defense is a mouthful of some fifty teeth, with a hiss and a growl, although they are nonaggressive and very shy. They feed off fruit, garbage bins, and the odd rodent that they can overcome.

Opossums travel alone and hide out in the day without permanent homes, which is probably where the expression "playing possum" originated. We rarely see them, but they are everywhere and flourish in the Valley.

Opossums' enemies are coyotes, bobcats, and dogs, and also cars and people who do not understand their harmless ways. They resist most diseases, such as rabies or distemper, and are immune to the venom of rattlesnakes. They do not dig or turn over trash cans or raid chicken coops, but will clean up edible trash left in backyards. The wise understand that if people knew opossums more completely, both would be better off, and the world would be much improved. And, by the way, these critters were named by the Algonquin Indian tribe as apasum, meaning "white animal." To be correct, the o found today should be pronounced with a slight "uh" sound to distinguish one as an opossum aficionado. Also, the males are "jacks," the females "jills," the young "joeys," and a bunch—a rare occurrence—a "passel."

Animal rescue people, vets, County of Santa Barbara Animal Services, and many residents know that the place for a wounded or distressed opossum is with Dawn the "Possum Lady," who after a call to (805) 688-5899 will be on the job. This is just one more dimension of our animal-oriented Valley, and one that should make us proud.

When Dawn received that call regarding the occupied Volkswagen, she responded immediately to the scene of the people–opossum standoff. The scampering joeys were easily corralled from under the hood and boxed, but the mother proved more difficult. The trick in such a situation is to immobilize the many-teethed mouth with a cloth and then muscle the distressed mother into an awaiting box. But in this instance, the opossum retreated and squirmed into the recesses of the engine compartment. Finally, after an hour of grab and scamper, the rescue capture was accomplished, but not before Dawn and interloper were liberally lathered with black engine grease.

The tourist couple now continued on their way, and Dawn brought the opossum family to her home for nursing care. The process of engine oil cleaning and recuperation took only three days in this case, and the goodbyes were said upon opening the nesting box in the country, down by the Santa Ynez River. Opossums swim, but that afternoon, sensing the person meant no harm, the rescued marsupial mother just casually wandered into the brush, with her babies following and scampering around her—making this a happy day for both opossums and the "Possum Lady," Dawn Summerlin.

Hoot Hurt

When Casey DeFranco received a call from her neighbor alerting her to a wounded owl in her driveway, she knew immediately to call her friend Ann Clausen, who would know what to do.

Ann is one of those prized Valley characters who symbolize the sympathetic attitude of our residents for aiding animals in need. Her specialty is wounded birds, although she will apply her good instincts to any hurt creature. Large, injured birds are usually deprived of their ability to fly but still able to strike back with beak and claw, and the capture and transport of a hurt raptor is not for everyone. Ann's weapon of choice is a favorite, first-strike, beach towel, backed up with secondary wrapping towels. She never uses gloves or gauntlets, but rather trusts her instincts and experience to subdue an angry bird who does not understand her good intentions.

When Ann arrived at the DeFranco scene, she took charge and, with Casey screaming and dodging in the background, soon cornered the grounded owl. A wounded, drooping wing prevented it from flying, but it could scamper quickly, highly motivated with survival instinct, and with no idea of the good purpose of its rescuers. The fierce-looking big bird seemed somewhat disoriented, finally taking a defensive position against a wire mesh fence, on its back with claws and beak ready to strike.

Ann quickly and expertly toweled the head to disarm the beak and followed immediately with a second towel around the clawed feet, and a third to swaddle and immobilize the now completely wrapped owl. A dash into a carrying box, and the first stage of rescue was complete.

Ann Clausen is not connected to any organization or authority, but is well known by Santa Barbara County animal rescue people, veterinarians, sheriffs, and animal-savvy residents. A large, angry, hurt raptor is a very specialized patient, and when a hawk, eagle, bat, or owl is reported, Ann is ready to volunteer. The ultimate medical care destination for a wounded bird is firstly Santa Barbara Wildlife Care Network, an organization of volunteers who will apply first-aid and sometimes rehabilitation to any hurt creature. The next step for birds might be the Ojai Raptor Center, where major treatment and rehabilitation is accomplished before returning restored patients to the wild.

Ann has been summoned for all manner of animal rescue. Once, a fancy bridesmaids' party taking place at a winery made a panic call for rescue from a bat attack. (Bats like wineries.) Ann arrived with towel protection to find an overturned box trapping the threatening bat and the lacy-dressed party huddled defensively in a corner. Expecting to find a Transylvanian killer, she cautiously turned the box up to discover a baby bat, not quite one inch long! The infant did not survive, and the relieved party, with blood veins intact, happily returned to the Chardonnay.

Another time, Ann was called to the beach beyond Vandenberg Air Force Base to rescue a wounded heron. A short chase on the shore, which the beach ranger wanted no part of, brought the towel-wrapped bird safely under control with the fierce, spear-like beak disarmed. But that did not prevent the hurting bird from broadcasting a heroic heron howl straight out of Jurassic Park. This was clearly a case for Santa Barbara Wildlife Care

Network. When Ann arrived, the somewhat officious attendant began to take the bird without messy towel protection. She quickly explained that herons sport a fierce and hurtful poke by flexing their long necks and striking with their pointy beak. Her advice was not accepted, but proved all too true when howls of pain and ugly language were heard from the back room. The heron survived, and the Wildlife Care Network people were pleased to send it on its way with repaired wing.

A more gratifying incident was a distress call from a young girl's birthday party. A baby owl had been discovered below a large oak tree, healthy, but unable to fly. Ann arrived at the scene, cradled the owl infant, and found no injury. She followed her instinct and, with the help of a stepladder, placed the owlet high in a fork in the branches. Some vibration caused her to look up in the tree, and sure enough, there was big momma owl following her every move with huge, penetrating owl eyes. After a hasty retreat, all was well in the nest. This was a happy ending, but not all her stories end that way.

The owl rescued from Casey DeFranco's driveway, identified as "SBWCN #2910," was forwarded from the Wildlife Care Network in Goleta to the Ojai Raptor Center, where specialists have a great track record for restoring wounded birds. In this case, however, although the wing was not found to be broken, the cockeyed look in the eyes had betrayed an internal brain injury, which caused the unfortunate owl to die.

Uncle Monty

With all of Monty Roberts's national and international recognition and world-championship wins, along with his racing skills (see "Bittersweet Racing" herein), it might seem strange that he would spend his nonexistent spare time rescuing orphan deer. However, in his mind, a queen of England investiture as a member of the Royal Victorian Order, honorary doctorates from the Universities of Zurich and Parma, and horseracing the world over all become secondary to his skills in foundling fawn rescue. But that is who he is, and a number of now-happy local deer remember him fondly for their early care, feeding, and affection.

For years, the California Highway Patrol and Department of Fish and Wildlife authorities have known that if they come across an orphan fawn, they can drop it off with Monty and Pat Roberts at Flag Is Up Farms between Solvang and Buellton. The little tykes will then have a chance at survival without upbringing by their mother deer, killed by a road accident. The orphans will then live to be released in the herds that roam the Santa Ynez Valley.

Since 1989, Monty's "Return to the Wild" program has seen many rescues. Linda and Sid Kastner once brought Monty a fawn they had discovered alone and failing on their Happy Canyon ranch. They had fed it yogurt, which the startled foundling lapped up like mother's milk and so had been given the nickname "Yoplait." After a stay at the Roberts ranch, the stranded deer lived to join the herd. A Lompoc-based Fish and Wildlife warden brought in an orphan fawn rescued from coyotes whom Monty named "Bambo" after Disney's famed Bambi. Our animal godfather likewise released that lucky survivor back to the wild. There have been many such rescues, but one stands out with particular attachment to the otherwise worldly author, lecturer, and horse-training icon.

One early evening, incidentally on his birthday, May 14, Monty was walking on his ranch and came across a proud mother deer with two twin offspring in tow. To his surprise, he then noticed a third pint-size creature trying to keep up, but with very little chance of survival in the real world. Deer triplets are rare but possible; unfortunately, however, the competition among a threesome with only a "two spigot" mother results in the weakest falling behind and becoming coyote bait. But here, Uncle Monty responded to the family runt, and the weak fawn responded to his new and only friend.

The fawn allowed Monty to cradle him and bring him home to Pat, who helped organize a bottle of warm baby-human milk formula. Pat knew the routine and her husband's predilections, and made it clear that if the frail orphan was joining the family Monty was on his own with the upbringing chores. This care, with the consultation of a sympathetic veterinarian, involved a complicated combination of bottle-feeding every two hours for the first month, and careful feeding and maintenance thereafter, until the tiny orphan reached healthy young deer size and strength. Meanwhile, the animal had completely bonded with Monty; had recognized him as his mother, father, and everything; and cuddled, nuzzled, and licked the happy horse trainer, showering love and affection. And that was all Monty needed to maintain the schedule and demands of a deer family man.

It so happens that the queen of England enjoys a transatlantic chat with Monty from time to time, and in the course of conversation, Monty related the story of their new and growing family member. "Ma'am, you are good at horse naming, so perhaps you could give me a name for this young buck-to-be."

"Monty!" the Queen exclaimed. "You must call him 'Benediction' because you are a blessing to him and he, with his acceptance and love, is a blessing to you!" So Benediction, or "Benny" for short, it was, and he was christened and grew into a healthy member of the herd.

The realities of nature are that, unlike the many dogs that have graced Monty and Pat's life, deer do not grow up to be household family members. As Benny grew and prospered, seeking life in the hillside herd was a natural progression, and deer and dad inevitably went their separate ways. But Monty will forever hold fond dreams of an affectionate and demanding rescue and helping one of God's creatures into the world.

This episode well illustrates the Valley disposition, where one who has achieved international fame and success can bottle-feed a fawn every two hours, enjoy the nuzzles of a devoted creature, and experience the fulfillment and contentment of this labor of love.

Christmas Count

In the late 1800s, American communities developed the tradition of household breadwinners going out with their shotguns in competition with each other to see who could shoot the most edible birds to bring home for the larder. The one who bagged the most had bragging rights and probably more food than the family could consume. But even then, the noble inclination for conservation guided our traditions, and soon weapons were replaced with pencil and paper and shots with spottings of bird varieties and quantities. On Christmas Day in 1900, the first recorded "Christmas Bird Count" took place, and the annual counting event has grown and energized ever since.

An important day in many bird-watchers' lives, the count occurs around the world now, and also serves as an annual environmental barometer. The count takes place on five separate days over a period of two weeks around Christmas, ending January 5. Santa Barbara County is divided into five "circles," each with a radius of 7.5 miles: Santa Maria/Guadalupe, La Purisima/Lompoc, the Santa Barbara city area, Carpinteria, and our Valley, designated as the "Cachuma Circle." In 2019, the Valley portion of the count took place on December 27.

Once the date and circles of the county bird count are established, the areas to be covered are planned out with an organizer and volunteers to cover each sector. This December 27, 2019, I was privileged to join the team assigned to the University of California's Sedgwick Reserve section of the Cachuma Circle count.

The organizer, Andy Lentz, brought the group of birders together on a cold dawn at the windy Anderson Overlook point. About nine birders gathered by car, well bundled against the cold, and greeted each other as old friends while focusing their binoculars and cocking their ears. The first birdcalls and sightings were soon recorded from the promontory, but there was a large territory to cover and the challenge of the count required the group to split up in pairs and walk or drive their sectors. In the distance, we watched a hawk being "mobbed" by a group of defending birds, which was only the beginning of my amateur eye-opening sightings as the welcome sun rose on that morning.

The count had officially begun in the dark of night, with Andy Lentz and Dennis Nord stalking and identifying three great horned owls and one barn owl. These four were noted in their records and began what was hoped to be a prolific day on the Reserve.

I immediately sensed that if the world became populated with only birders, we would be much better off. The general description of the

Valley group, typical of most birders, reads something like this: friendly, thoughtful, environmental, supportive, unthreateningly intellectual, and somewhat balmy. Birders have keen eyes that can pick out a fluff of feathers in a distant tree or soaring shapes in the atmosphere. They can hear distant cheeping sounds that escape normal ears and identify a bird variety by a greeting tweet or mating song from a far-off branch. Some birders are experts, and some beginner types need to consult books and apps for each spotting. Many birders keep a "life list" of all the species they have individually spotted, and some only wander, watch, and take in the fresh air.

Years ago my favorite cousin was dating a Washington, DC, character, a very pleasant man who worked for the Central Intelligence Agency. We had no idea what he did in his spooky world, but when he visited us in the Santa Ynez Valley, we discovered his passion was bird-watching. He had not been to the Valley before, and all he wanted to do was hike the hills with his binoculars and add to his life list of birds that he personally had spotted. I had always admired our yellow-billed magpies for their beautiful black-and-white coloring and their quirky bird mannerisms. However, this visitor's ecstatic viewing of our local magpies—and my seeing these brightly colored and strutting critters through his eyes as he spotted one for the first time in his career—was a revelation. To experience his excitement on seeing his first yellow-billed magpie added a whole new dimension to the local bird's persona. This visiting spotter introduced me to a bird I had only casually known, and magpies have been a joy to behold ever since.

Bird-watchers develop a keen sense of sight and instinct to search out birds hidden from the rest of us. "See that woodpecker in the high branch of the third oak down from the crest?" one helpful watcher on the Sedgwick bird count trail said as he offered his high-intensity binoculars. Well, maybe the bird was watching me, but I never saw its distant black-and-white plumage with a dash of red markings.

I was lucky to be assigned to a four-wheeled vehicle equipped with a welcome heater and piloted by Kate McCurdy, the University of California, Santa Barbara's Sedgwick Reserve manager. She is an avid birder, knows the Reserve intimately, and told a host of good stories as we searched our sector. She spotted birds that I could either lie about seeing or confess my blindness to, but as time went on, I began to see flying critters I never would have noticed previously. I learned about birds, and began to understand the joys of bird-watching.

As we walked and drove that beautiful ranch, I may not have spotted many birds, but I did discover a new dimension of life: birding is fun. What more could one ask for in a hobby than good company, fresh air, exercise, and a healthy and harmless print on the environment while watching as many as possible of God's most beautiful creatures? Many of us, and particularly retired types, are seeking new friends, exercise, avocation, and mental stimulus. Birding fills all these needs and more.

Anyone interested can contact the Santa Barbara Museum of Natural History for classes and the Santa Barbara Audubon Society for scheduled bird walks, mentors, and even groups for seniors or young students. There are no rules or requirements, although a warm jacket, comfortable walking boots, binoculars, a bird picture book, and a writing pad will be of use. On a day's outing, one can find bird experts and skilled spotters and listeners as well as rank beginners squinting to the heavens. And best of all, one can find and learn to appreciate anything from an American crow to a bald eagle.

As mentioned, the Sedgwick count began in the near darkness with three great horned owls and a barn owl. The sightings grew in number as the birders fanned out and communicated their bird sightings to each other. A sage thrasher, a rare visitor to the ranch, was spotted by one alert birder. Toward the end of the day, three usual locals, a red-breasted sapsucker, a lark sparrow, and an American pipit, had not been spotted and were missing from the daily record. The group split up, redoubled their efforts, and finally added those three to the list. The last bird to be spotted was a golden eagle, a species that was usually seen on the ranch, but had been elusive until the group was almost ready to give in with the darkness.

Finally, the birders assembled for dinner and compilation at the Sedgwick ranch house. Our count on the Sedgwick Reserve, fifty-seven species, turned out by chance to be identical to the 2017 total, with one or two additions and one or two subtractions. The day had been long and initially cold, but was generally thought to be a successful outing. The bird population was holding steady and even prospering in that segment of our Valley, and the birders had a splendid day verifying the beautiful, flying and chirping population. Our fifty-seven-bird total would now be combined with those of the other observers in the Cachuma Circle and be reported to the National Audubon Society for inclusion in the Christmas Bird Count statistics.

The Christmas Bird Count compilation dinner for Santa Barbara County was held in the Fleischmann Auditorium on Saturday, January 4, the day of the greater Santa Barbara city area count. A threat of rain, which had the aspect of a snowstorm, caused a concern that the day might bring diminished returns, and the early-afternoon showers certainly affected the count in that last area. Birders are also worried that the drought in our region, leading to stressed and dying trees, might reduce the bird population. Plus, fires and landslides could threaten habitat in the southern portion of our county. But the final 2019 county tally was 197 species, a respectable number, though somewhat under the record high of 227.

The prize find for the Santa Barbara day was a long-eared owl, spotted roosting in a pepper tree. Two birders had noticed what they call "paint," otherwise known as bird poop, on the ground and, in looking up to find the source, had discovered this large, distinctive owl, which is seldom seen in the county. The assembled county birders reveled in the story of this rare find at the annual dinner.

One can only admire the enthusiasm and dedication of serious birders. But hearing of these dedicated birders can only help us appreciate our own sightings in parking lots or backyards. And, if by any chance we become involved further in birding, we will thank our good fortune to take part in this fascinating hobby.

· **F** ·

Counterfeit Bucks

The Sedgwick Reserve is a world-class research, conservation, and education facility of five-thousand-plus acres in the Santa Ynez Valley nestled below Figueroa Mountain and owned and managed by the University of California, Santa Barbara. The property was donated to the university in 1967 by one of our more colorful historic Valley characters, Francis "Duke" Sedgwick, and is dedicated to research, education, and arts programs. Of course, the nature of the property does not allow hunting— as the animals of the Valley who are stalked by hunters have come to know.

The fall deer-hunting season brings a threat to the antlered population from locals who have stocked their larders for generations, and also from many Los Angeles urban gunslingers, some of whom take their legal opportunity to bag a buck in the wild, but many of whom will shoot up any animal, anywhere, resembling a deer that crosses their path. The deer population senses this threat, and many find refuge in Sedgwick Reserve, where hunting is forbidden.

Some grand bucks seek shelter in the Sedgwick, and the herd swells in hunting season when gunshots can be heard from surrounding hills. The deer sanctuary is protected by Sedgwick policy and enforced by the California Department of Fish and Wildlife, whose officers take a very dim view of trespassing or poaching in any form. These "Warden Smokeys" in their green trucks prowl the back paths of our Valley applying strict hunting policy and assessing misdemeanors and fines on violators who hunt out of season or out of bounds.

One method of enforcement that has produced splendid stories and bagged many poachers is the use of decoys, often employed on the protected property of the Sedgwick. The decoy trap is set by carefully disguising and setting in place a mechanical buck, partly hidden in the brush some seventy-five to a hundred yards from a back road where hunting is prohibited. This tempting target is sometimes dressed as a single-horned young buck or even a doe, to compound the crime of illegal hunting. The realistic dummy is clothed in deerskin, planted in the ground with metal rods, and often sporting a mechanical apparatus that shakes the head at random, from side to side.

When the dummy deer is in place, a warden will hide near the decoy with a device to initiate the head wagging. Radio contact will be maintained with two other wardens in well-hidden trucks off the road on both directions from the setup. The warden detail will settle in and await developments.

Typically, some yahoos with a six-pack of beer and a high-powered rifle will drive along, spot the "deer," and aim to shoot from the vehicle. After a shot or two, the pair of deputy vehicles will arrive with lights and sirens shattering the wilderness and issue a citation to the amazed hunting crew. If the shooters have dismounted, then crossed a fence to gain a closer shot, they will have added a trespassing offense. If the "buck" happens to be dressed as a doe that day, they will have one more fine. The day will result in a strict lesson in hunting manners and technique and a court-ordered one- to five-thousand-dollar fine that any red-faced hunter will rarely, if ever, dispute. Sometimes two or three so-called hunters will learn the same hard lesson in a day, and the word will spread that hunting should only be done appropriately, and the Sedgwick is truly off-limits.

There are numerous stories of these encounters. Some hunters figure out the game after only one shot. Some will bang away a number of times, frustrated in their aim before meeting the wardens. Some will curse the wardens while they are writing the ticket, and some will laugh at their own stupidity. The decoys just take the shots without complaint, but an outstanding episode remains legend and is often told back at headquarters.

One day, a typical carload out for hunting thrills drove up the mountain road and stopped when they thought they had spotted a deer. True to form, the hidden warden was working the head-wagging device, while a rifle appeared out the back window and shot the mechanical deer in the neck. Somehow the motion device was sprung by the bullet, and the head continued to move back and forth. Frustrated by the misses, the gunner shot again and again. The "deer" just stood and shook his head, seeming to say, "Ouch, no, no, don't shoot me again." Finally, the rifle was empty, just before the wardens surrounded the car to arrest the frustrated shooter. Later, the would-be hunter met the prosecutor, paid his fine, and only hoped the story would never make the rounds.

On any day, visitors to the Sedgwick can make an appointment and enjoy one of the great scenic ranches in the Valley. When they see a healthy deer population, they will now know why.

Symbol Savers

The bald eagle holds U.S. symbol status for good reason. This majestic, compellingly beautiful bird soars the skies of our Valley with a stately, bold presence that is a fitting representation of our country's freedom and might.

The big birds are often found in the Lake Cachuma neighborhood and also fly in the oak foothills of the Valley. At least two families can be regularly seen in the vicinity of Foxen Canyon, just off Highway 101. One of these mighty birds lost all dignity and nearly its life one day in the

Saarloos ranch reservoir on Zaca Station Road.

Larry Saarloos and his employees had come to appreciate the occasional glimpse of a splendid pair of bald eagles soaring in the ranch vicinity, and enjoyed hearing their piercing calls. The nearly two-acre vineyard reservoir on the ranch contains eagle-food fish, but is circled by steep banks without footholds, resulting in a difficult exit.

I had experienced this problem in a previous year when walking on the ranch one hot afternoon with a Shepherd dog named Tucker. He had plunged into the reservoir for a refreshing dip, but was unable to scramble out of the water. As I was alone, I could only reassure my dog friend that help was on the way and wait until a backup arrived who could rope me down the bank so I could grab the dog and he could haul us both up the bank. Had Tucker been alone, he might not have survived, and had I attempted to help him without backup, I might have perished as well.

Bald eagles can be three feet high, weigh seven to eight pounds, and sport a wing span from five to over seven feet. Their piercing eyes and forceful presence well qualify them as our nation's symbol. They can live into their thirties, and the birds mate for life. Their hollow bones and the fluffy down under their feathers allow them to float, and by a clever motion of their wings, they can actually swim. But they cannot stay afloat forever.

Apparently one of the eagles had swooped into the reservoir after a fish and, though able to reach the bank, had not been able to climb out. Unlike, for instance, a pelican, eagles cannot take off from the water, and need to clamber out like people. Their preferred fishing technique would be the swoop and grab, but this eagle plunged and stayed in the water and, left to his own devices, would probably drown.

By good chance, the Saarloos ranch foreman, Pedro Rea, came along and noticed the floundering big bird struggling in the water. By more good chance, Pedro is a first-class roper and happened to have a rope in his truck. With care and skill, Pedro threw a loop onto the struggling eagle, slowly tightened the hold, and gently hauled the bird out of the water and up the bank.

There was no fight in the exhausted eagle as it lay almost comatose on the ground. Apparently just staying afloat for as long as he had been in the water took all the energy out of the soaking bird body, and the raptor hardly stirred as Pedro removed the noose. Pedro was even able to help the big bird stand upright and spread his sodden wings to the drying sun. Bird and man watched each other from a distance while the eagle stood straight with wings extended to dry the feathers and recover energy in the warmth of the day. Finally, after almost two hours, the bird moved forward and was able to take off.

Amazingly, the eagle pairs have remained in the area and are still seen by the Saarloos people. Surely Pedro's eagle is a wiser bird in fishing technique.

Larry and Harvey Saarloos told me this story reluctantly, knowing well the serious federal protection of bald eagles and the heavy enforcement hand of California Department of Fish and Wildlife authorities. We can only be sure that if this tale is told, the amateur protectionists and government officials will offer a medal and not a censure. This incident well illustrates the relationship between our ranchers and our resident animals.

Hunger Games

Most of us in the Valley have seen seemingly shy and inoffensive coyotes from time to time. Coyotes see us much more often, and these wily ones closely watch our household dogs and cats with dinnertime in mind. Cats regularly disappear in the night, and even small and large dogs are hunted regularly.

I well remember a scene from when we lived at the winery on a wide flat field. I walked out on our porch, with very lucky timing, to see our large Shepherd dog, Tucker, belly-to-the-ground chasing a coyote. A moment later, I noticed a second coyote full-out running behind Tucker!

Our dog had fallen into a coyote pack trap, and instead of being the chaser, Tucker was about to be very much the chased, and perhaps the victim of a clever coyote hunting technique. I yelled my lungs out and rang a bell we had hanging on the porch. Somehow that turned the attention of the coyote–dog chase, and Tucker came home to my call. All was well, with no coyote supper, but such confrontations are not unusual in our Valley.

In another attack, a former Valley couple, Tony and Elizabeth Hirsch, were peacefully dining in their home when their Jack Russell Terrier, Roxy, screamed for help from the driveway. Elizabeth was first on the scene and diverted the attention of three coyotes about to maul the small, terrified dog. The saving of the day was actually effected by Tony, who, in dashing to the rescue, ran into a screen door with a loud bang that startled and scared the coyotes, who disappeared into the brush. Peace returned to the Hirsch home as Roxy licked her (fortunately) light wounds, Tony nursed his bruises, and Liz poured herself a glass of wine.

The Alisal Guest Ranch & Resort residential properties are surrounded by bands of coyotes who often intrude on homesteads, hoping to score a family cat or dog. One notable incident nearly cost a friendly, dopey Golden Retriever named Frankie his life. The dog, part of the Weiner family, lived happily and comfortably on the warm hearth, fenced off from the world, except when he could escape and roam. One afternoon, he cut loose and meandered to an adjoining hillside, running about and sniffing ground squirrel holes scattered on the cattle-grazing ranchland.

By good fortune, a neighbor, Jen Sanregret, happened to be in her backyard, playing with her children. They too were on the edge of the Alisal Guest Ranch cattle pasture, and from time to time noticed coyotes wandering on that sidehill. Coyotes often came near the Sanregret home, and challenged their dogs, but were well separated by a chain-link fence. Fortunately for the carefree Frankie, Jen was a Texas girl, wise and suspicious of coyote ways. By good chance, she spotted one quietly closing in on the frolicking dog, and immediately sensed the danger.

She ran out of the house, leaving the kids to her startled husband, Grant, and jumped into her car to drive to the suspicious dog–coyote scene. She pulled over just down the road at the pasture barbwire fence. Sure enough, not one but three coyotes were slowly closing in on the unsuspecting Golden Retriever. Jen had the sense of a Disney film about to go bad—a happy-go-lucky, friendly dog strolling on the green grass, and three sinister coyotes slinking into surrounding, lethal striking positions. She called and urged the friendly dog to come to her at the fence.

Finally, Frankie raised his head and noticed the coyote threat. He dashed for Jen, and the coyotes actually followed the now-terrified dog toward his rescuer. He reached the fence, and Jen dragged him through, leaving golden fur on some of the fence barbs. The two scrambled into the waiting car.

The coyotes must have been young, or at least very hungry for dog dinner, because they normally never come close if a human is involved. The barbwire fence seemed to draw a line, because they stopped short and backed off, but not before coming within a dozen feet of Jen dragging the dog!

Dog and rescuer drove back home, where a righteously indignant Grant exclaimed, "You just did what?!" Jen drove the chastened Frankie back to an amazed Jon and Joanna Weiner. And all finally settled down in the neighborhood, including coyotes back in their hideaway.

Just as an added thought, for those of us neighbors who love dogs more than coyotes, discharging a firearm in Solvang is worth a trip to the municipal court!

Academic Rattles

A long-held standard that I have used to judge the worst-possible human activity came from a magazine article I once read about an ardent biologist's doctoral thesis on hibernation. This young man trudged the cold winter mountains of Alaska seeking caves containing hibernating bears. He then crawled in with them and somehow obtained their rectal temperatures to document their hibernating physical characteristics. He survived, but still has dreams. That is my standard for worst, and another local activity at first seemed to be a close second.

As a master's candidate at California Polytechnic State University, Hayley Crowell undertook a rattlesnake study that initially seemed

appalling but later, after I learned the details, opened my mind to a more positive acceptance of our beady-eyed Valley snakes. The study—"Comparative Thermal Ecology of Coastal and Inland Pacific Rattlesnakes (Crotalus oreganus)"—required her to capture these reptiles from the Sedgwick Reserve, transport them to Cal Poly where a thermal recording and broadcast radio transmitter device was surgically inserted, and then release the startled animals back where they came from. The inserted device enabled her to record daily changes in their body temperature.

The first volume of Valley Animals included an episode titled "Close Call" outlining various events that portrayed the rattlers as villains, but a long interview with Hayley, describing her relationship with rattlesnakes while pursuing her thesis, led me to a more charitable and positive view of the snakes. Her knowledge of and relationship with them demonstrates that while rattlers might be fanged at one end and rattled at the other, they also possess a place in the panoply of God's creatures, and a defensive innocence that belies our instinctual fear and loathing. They want to eat, but otherwise have no evil intentions about any passing animals or people.

Our local rattlesnakes spend their days lying in the grass in benign somnolence, saving their precious venom-weapon fangs for the occasional kill, enjoyed only a few times a year for subsistence. Ground squirrels are the meal of choice. The reptiles fear almost anything else that might be a predator, particularly large birds, passing boars, or stealthy king snakes, all of whom make a living off the sleepy, sunning rattlers. They will quietly ignore or flee anything large and threatening, particularly humans, hoping that these strangers will not see through their clever camouflage. Many local hikers and ranchers probably come closer to rattlers more often than they realize when the snakes simply remain silent. But usually, if threatened, an alarmed snake will rattle to frighten an intruder and then strike only as a last resort. A clumsy predator might be tempted to attack the noisy back end and suffer a deadly surprise from the weaponized front end.

The incidence of snakebite is surprisingly low in the Valley, with many more dog bites than snakebites. In an average year, only one or two cases of snakebite are rushed to our Santa Ynez Valley Cottage Hospital. Sometimes the bite has been delivered by an angry gopher snake, not a rattler, and sometimes the venom has not been delivered severely enough to cause concern. Our local Cottage Hospital branch has recorded some treatments with the antivenom CroFab®, but never any deaths from rattler bites. On the Sedgwick Reserve, where Hayley carried out her research, visitors have more chance of being treed by a wild boar than being bitten by a snake.

Hayley's research required her to walk the Sedgwick, always with a partner, to find and capture rattlesnakes. She wore boots and protective leggings, but no gloves, and wielded a long snake-seizing device with a transporting bucket. Her knowledge of snake lore is amazing, and where most would walk the ranch seeing no snakes, she knows where they lie and how to find and capture them with ease. She admires and respects snakes, and they hold no threat or mystery to her.

Hayley views rattlesnakes as an important ingredient in our environment. They do not hibernate, are very social, make good mothers, and take good care of their young. The males wrestle but do not bite each other, they carry no disease, they are quiet, and, above all, they keep the ground squirrel population in check. Hayley's thesis, relying on the transmitted body temperatures from the devices implanted in the snakes, provides information about and explains how rattlers seek optimum comfort at around 30 degrees Celsius, and explores if, indeed, that is their most favored body temperature. Ultimately, this study might have implications for climate change and its possible effect on the habits of snakes. With explorations that also involve rattlesnakes from the Carrizo Plain National Monument, Vandenberg Air Force Base, and Montaña de Oro State Park, Hayley is discovering a somewhat obscure, but significant, dimension of our ecology that will be of substantial importance to our understanding of climate, species adaption, and the life and times of rattlesnakes.

The Valley might not fully appreciate the usefulness of her information concerning the body temperature of rattlesnakes. However, we can celebrate the hard work of a young master's degree candidate and learn something from her understanding of a mostly misunderstood Valley reptile. All of this may be reassuring and dispel many fears and incorrect notions of rattlers, but it is totally understandable if readers do not wish one for a pet.

Turkey Trots

Turkeys are rare in the wild, especially on legal hunting days, but one flock has found a happy home at the Alisal Guest Ranch & Resort. One- to three-dozen of these stately birds roam the homes and hills of the ranch with great aplomb and mixed acceptance. Drivers can hardly believe their eyes as they stop for a herd sauntering across the road.

Wild turkeys are happy in California. They somehow almost became extinct in ancient times, but have proliferated to over 18 percent of our state. They run in herds, weigh around twenty pounds each, and make gentle guttural clucks and coos that convey a kind of remote satisfaction. A community such as the Alisal is a perfect home, with flowers and gardens to gobble, roofs to occupy, and occasionally a sympathetic homeowner who will supply delicious treats. Such turkey encouragement is very much discouraged by ranch management because the birds are not without problems.

Turkey poop can be very smelly and abundant. An unlucky home, determined to be a nightly roost, is soon to be unbearable. Turkeys rarely become aggressive, but do have that potential. If there is a need to shoo them off a yard, it is good to go armed with a broom or even an umbrella. Once, while walking along Alisal Road, I encountered a charming new neighbor whom I had wanted to meet anyway. She seemed alarmed, and was warily eyeing a turkey herd that was strutting its way just off the road. "Will they attack?" she asked. I assured her that they are aggressive only when one walks alone, and thereby gained a pleasant walking companion.

My wife, Kate, was enjoying the company of two Shepherd-type dog friends when she noticed an overpopulated herd encroaching on our grounds. She set the dogs on the birds to shoo them back onto the open Alisal country, but her lady–dog effort went only as far as a bird retreat to our neighbor's yard, with the natural-born herding dogs no help at all. Finally, after the turkeys had retreated, the dogs, with all their herding instincts, came alive. The two Shepherds set off with inbred vigor, rounded up the birds, and brought them smartly back into our yard. Birds were disgruntled and edgy, dogs were proud and looking for approval, and Kate was unhappy with the entire scene.

The big birds are prey for coyotes and mountain lions, but able to fly away into the trees if there is adequate warning. They are also able to run quickly if too lazy to take flight. They safely tuck themselves in at night to roost in trees or on rooftops, and thereby present a problem. A warm roof is a desirable roost, but their biological waste soon takes over. One elderly lady (whose name shall remain undisclosed) was driven to distraction by the herd routinely lodging on her eaves. A helpful and creative grandson fetched a bow and arrow and lanced one of the toms who then had to be dispatched by a neighbor with a shovel. The same shovel was quickly employed to hide the evidence from searching Fish and Wildlife authorities or a resident representative of People for the Ethical Treatment of Animals. The incident did serve to discourage future boarders, who took their turkey poop elsewhere.

Alisal Guest Ranch managers have a mixed view of the birds, and concluded that proportionality is important. A few birds are scenic and acceptable; many birds are a pain in the ass. Accordingly, the cowboys and groundskeepers of the ranch have come up with a system, beginning with distributing delectable grain pickings around a certain open corral. Periodically, the turkeys will happily meander into the enclosure and enjoy a meal, and one day, a large, innocent-looking trailer will back up into the area, but not in a way that alarms the herd.

Over time, the turkeys will continue to enjoy the grain put down in the enclosure and routinely show up for the feast. Later, however, they will come to discover that the grain has been placed in the trailer—from which, with a turkey shrug, the birds will eventually feed. But then the back gate of the trailer will snap shut, and a good part of the herd will be off to a sympathetic ranch out on Highway 246. The birds will be perfectly happy in the Santa Rita Hills, but might wonder where the roofs, dogs, and ladies with brooms have disappeared to.

Visitors to the Valley are charmed to see the ancient, stately birds making their unique way alongside our roads, and thereby learn the happy partnership of birds and people.

Part Two

COMMERCIAL ENTERPRISE

Show Business

Many locals have enjoyed watching Ramon Becerra perform and watching his horses do things people never expect these animals to do. Ramon has a rare talent for communicating with horses performing to delight audiences. He is a Valley regular who is worth knowing, or at least whose acts are worth watching.

Ramon has made his career touring the country, hired to perform in rodeos, horse shows, and similar arena events. He will be introduced and, with a smile on his face, accomplish moves with his trained horses that fill in the gaps of competition events. For example, one signature act is to have a horse lie down with his head resting on the ground. Ramon then will stand on top of the horse and do rope tricks for as long as the event manager needs. Sometimes the audience enjoys Ramon more than the competition events, but other times his entertainments do not go smoothly.

Once, at a large horse show in the East, he had one horse lie down and another stand crossways over the one lying flat out, and then he climbed to stand high on the saddle to perform rope tricks. He was in the middle of an outside show ring with a large audience watching from the stands, a typical scene of his show business career. But on this occasion he noticed in the middle of his act that the flat-out horse seemed somewhat agitated. From his position standing high on the saddle, he could do little except make calming noises to the twitching horse below. But the distress in the horse's eyes and his shaking head demonstrated that something was definitely going wrong. If the supine horse began to flail up, the three would be a tumbled mess. Finally, Ramon clambered down, stepped off and over the upright horse, and helped the downed horse get up. Only then did he see that a nearby gopher had been busily shoveling dirt out of a hole near the reclining horse's downed head, sprinkling the flat-out animal! He jumped on the now-upright mount and grabbed the reins of his standing horse, and the three cantered out of the ring to the cheers of a delighted audience. The unimpressed gopher continued his business.

Ramon comes from San Julián in the Mexican state of Jalisco. Early on, he seemed to be a natural, riding and training horses, and developed an impressive ability for rope tricks. He also has an engaging appeal to audiences with his smile and casual exhibition. Competition somehow never interested him, although riding and performing with horses fit his talents perfectly. As a young man, he toured with the Andalusian and Arabian horse string that had become a symbol of the world-famous Pedro Domecq brand of beverages, much as the Budweiser Clydesdales are a symbol of the beer brand. He toured America with these spirited Domecq horses, and this somehow brought him to meet John Derek, husband of our Valley favorite Bo Derek, and that brought a move to his home in Santa Ynez.

In his all-out show business days, he would drive the country with his talented string of horses and perform in major events. For instance, he was a regular for a two-week horse show, the famous Bridgehampton Classic in Long Island, doing his act once or twice a day to amazed audiences. He led an unusual life with a unique horse act, but it suited him and brought him a good living.

Once, in a large show, he performed a wild, war-painted Indian act. He was to fake being shot down on the ground, and his faithful horse was trained to come when called and rescue him. In recent years Ramon has begun to wear his hair long and braided, but in those early years he had to wear a wig that had long braids to complete his Indian costume. Unfortunately, when the horse came to the rescue, he stood on the braid, pinning Ramon to the ground, and would not budge. Horse and actor were at a standoff in the middle of the ring until finally the wig came off, and a scalped Indian jumped on the horse and sped off to the delight of the audience.

One of his fondest memories is serving as the driver for a carriage pulling the famous singer, Pepe Aguilar, and his beautiful daughter, Ángela, in parades. One can imagine the horse sense necessary to control a team pulling a loudly singing star through adoring, singing, and clapping fans. Ramon just seems to know what is going on in a horse's head.

Like most trainers, he admits that he cannot read a horsey mind, but does know how to work and train one. He somehow has the ability to sense which horse will cooperate. Some of his candidates will learn a trick in a week, some two months, some six months, and some never, but patience and animal sense pay off and mostly prevail. In all his career he has only had one bad accident, and that only recently when a stallion kicked him. The orthopedic surgeon who set his arm congratulated the horse on a perfectly clean break.

In one act, he turns his horse loose and runs him around the edge of the arena and then calls him back to be mounted. Once, in a big show, his reliable horse just decided to keep on running. After seven complete circuits, with Ramon calling plaintively and the horse breezing by a hundred miles an hour, the panting animal finally slowed and sidestepped to be mounted to the delight of the spectators.

Ramon has been the Marlboro Man many times for commercials that are now only made for overseas audiences. He fit the rugged cowboy picture perfectly, and of course the riding was no problem, but he did have a drawback in not being a smoker. He had to learn how to handle cigarettes and fake the smoking thing, but the pay is good, and the film people are easy to work with.

His most recent and well-paid gig was for a Gucci commercial. Here he had to coax horses to ride in cars, sit at lunch tables, ride through garden parties, and even share an apple bite with beautiful models. Many cowboys might wish for that assignment.

Currently, Ramon Beccera lives happily in Santa Ynez, and does not travel as often. He will perform for guests at the weekly Alisal Guest Ranch & Resort rodeos and for charity events. He is a totally sympathetic person to meet for either Valley residents or Valley horses, and has helped many of us with our horse problems.

· 🅕 ·

Trendy Creatures

Valley animals come in many shapes and sizes. Domestic cats, dogs and birds, ranch horses and cattle, and miscellaneous wild things roaming the hills and flying the skies all make up a great normal population of God's creatures. But to complete the inventory, we must add the occasional species that somehow becomes a center of emotional, economic, and irrational exuberance—a rush for owning, coveting, and investing. The periodic notions about these chosen creatures are hard to explain and fascinating to observe. Arabian horses, ostriches, alpacas, and potbellied pigs come to mind as the trends of the day, each with its moment of fame.

The classic hysterical investment craze that serves as an example was the Dutch tulip mania back in the 1600s. Tulip bulbs were irrationally bought and sold for fortunes; then suddenly the market collapsed and the bulbs returned to their garden value. Investors who did not get out in time went bankrupt. In the ensuing years, various real estate schemes, stocks, and commodities have experienced boom and bust, and our Valley has also seen a number of animal mania cycles.

The Arabian horse craze hit our Valley in the 1970s. These beautiful, prancing, exotic horses were bred and shown, bought and sold, and graced Valley paddocks while climbing to startling prices. Everyone seemed to want a flighty-minded Arabian in their pasture. Auction sales became the social events of the day and the money-burning means to own the beauties.

The Nichols-DeLongpre ranch on Cachuma Lake seen from Highway 154 hosted an annual star-studded extravaganza where Champagne and symphony orchestra accompanied Arabian horseflesh, paraded on spotlighted stages, with full-out show business special effects. Tens and even hundreds of thousands of dollars were bid in formal auction, as the shiny horses came to grace fancy stables around the country and Valley paddocks.

There was no sudden crash in the Arabian mania, but gradually the heavily promoted and comely horse breed lost luster and value, and the Valley Arabian farm population of these beauties settled back to normal sensibility. Still, a few diehard breeders are hanging on around 2020, but the star power and big bucks have long deserted the trend.

In the 1980s, ostriches became the rage. Stories of fortunes to be made from a herd of these large semi-birds abounded. A fertile egg was said to be worth hundreds of dollars, and visions of ostrich protein replacing hamburgers and a feather boa in every closet fueled Valley ranch dreams. Sometimes another exotic species of bird, the emu, augmented the herds.

Ranch hands learned the hard way about the dangers and personality disorders of these awkward birds. Training or even limited interaction with humans is just about nonexistent and sometimes downright deadly with these long-necked, long-legged, bird-brained heavyweights. If a person gets between a flirting female and an inspired male, or a hungry bird and ready chow, the result might be a lethal slash from a claw-foot that can even bring down a horse. The defense if a human is caught in that bind is to lie down flat on the ground, out of high-necked ostrich line of vision. Apparently out of sight is out of mind, and the daffy ostrich mind quickly forgets any dispute, ensuring the prone figure is safe to crawl away. I have actually spoken to an ostrich breeder who survived in that manner.

But once again, the boom settled back when the two or three restaurants that featured ostrich burgers experienced flagging orders from the menu, and the expected boa craze never crazed.

The interesting remains of the defunct Valley ostrich boom is called OstrichLand USA on Highway 246 east of Buellton. Here, a few-dozen ostriches happily beckon tourists to stop and meet an exotic species close up. A dollar is well spent on feeding the birds and experiencing their energy and bird determination. Most visitors are not pecked by the muscular beaks, and when a beak strike happens, it rarely breaks the skin and only leaves a bruise. Even a casual look-in will discover a friendly-seeming, big-eyed bird, but ostrich mingling is definitely not advised. Otherwise, OstrichLand is a hoot, even for locals.

The next rage came around the turn of the century when the Valley found alpacas. These lovable creatures that call the mountains of Peru home are good for one coat of super fiber each year that will produce the best sweaters in the world. Otherwise the shy woolies just hang around, poop splendid garden fertilizer, and emit tuneful grunting noses. People whom alpacas come to trust can give them a rewarding hug. Those who breed the herd will enjoy cute little spindly-legged offspring fuzzies, called cria, running around quite happily and looking like a Disney movie.

The sheared fiber, like Arabian conformation or ostrich fluff, can become an obsession with alpaca aficionados. Shows and auctions judge the worth of the splendid producers of wooly fiber and present trophies and ribbons to festoon the barn walls of breeders. At the height of the craze, champions might command thousands for breeding, and the silky-fleeced offspring of champions, with soft touch and a pure color, were coveted as would be a Kentucky Derby winner.

For a few years, alpacas were bought, sold, and bred, and graced the paddocks of small Valley holdings. Who could resist these big-eyed friendlies? Some even bought alpacas to be boarded at ranches just for visits and boasting rights.

The alpaca cycle never became a true boom or bust because prices never grew too ridiculous and the animals retained an intrinsic sheared-fiber value. As the trendy phase eased off, the animals were still easy to keep, still lovable, and still practical by way of the clothing they produced. Today, in 2020, those who bought at the height of the craze are hurting, but some reasonably valued herds still just graze away happily to the Valley ranches' satisfaction.

Potbellied pigs roam in the wild in Vietnam and found their way to the United States with other refugees in the 1970s and early '80s. These creatures lead benign lives, grunting and foraging, but much misunderstanding of their basic nature has led to unhappiness for both people and pigs. A newborn will weigh in at 2 or 3 pounds in friendly, cuddly, and appealing form. Soon, however, the porcine lovables grow into 125- to 200-pound consumption machines with definite needs. One knowledgeable potbellied-pig person said, "Dogs have a nature that wants to please a person. Pigs have a nature that wants to be pleased by a person."

Some ascribe the initiation of the potbellied pig craze to actor George Clooney, who bought a small, adorable baby pig in 1988, with all the usually star-studded publicity, and is noted for such quotes as "Love me, love my pig." Clooney had a friendly relationship with his pig, named Max, and always talked about him, but admits, as his father, Nick Clooney, wrote, "No one had told George that Max would grow to the size of a linebacker with an appetite to match."

Clooney complained that Max "was eating his way through life. I'd put him on a diet, but he screams like hell if he's not able to stuff himself the way he likes." Max lived happily with Clooney for eighteen years and finally topped out at over 300 pounds. When Max died, Clooney was asked if he would ever consider a new pig friend. "No," Clooney replied. "I think Max covered all my pig needs."

But the misconceptions about potbellied pigs and the celebrity-driven obsession with owning one has remained to the present. Sue Parkinson, a Valley animal saint who runs a potbellied pig rescue foundation called Lil' Orphan Hammies, has a long history of sad stories regarding unwanted, abandoned, and mistreated pigs, many of which have come under her care. People just do not understand that the cuddly cuties grow up big-time and have big needs. The sometimes-unscrupulous purveyors of these small creatures often mislead potential customers about the animals while charging up to a couple thousand dollars for a "prize teacup" potbellied baby. The celebrity star gets a story and a photograph, and then what? The "what" is often a call to Sue Parkinson.

Sue's Valley facility houses, cares, and dispenses advice for the care of unwanted pigs. She bemoans the sales gimmicks that dupe buyers into believing these animals will remain miniature house pets. A typical family will buy a potbellied pig and then watch in horror as the innocent animal follows a normal growth pattern into a demanding, albeit friendly, boarder with two speeds: lazy ways and urgent food demands. When the pigs top out at over 100 pounds, the household might call County Animal Services, abandon the pet on a back road, or call Lil' Orphan Hammies. Recently Sue Parkinson let me hear her phone mail, and there were too many calls asking for help in housing an unwanted pig. County Animal Services often requests her to house a pig, and one day she even brought in thirty-two potbellied pigs from another county. Her answer to the problem is publicity and knowledge about the realities of pig ownership.

Potbellied pigs are happy campers and pleasant boarders if there is space and owner understanding. Three or four contented potbellies could easily cohabit a five-acre ranch typically found in the Valley, where porcine life fits easily and socially with a family. The pigs will root and laze and mooch for more, but otherwise be happy cohabitants and round off the people–animal social traditions of the Valley. Sue Parkinson and her Lil' Orphan Hammies foundation will happily offer advice and adoption possibilities. Many Valley families will benefit from the vibrations of happy potbellied pig partners, but only if both understand the realities of cohabitation.

Currently, 2020 seems to be without a trendy animal craze in the Valley, and the people–animal balance seems to be on an even keel. Perhaps an understanding of the realities of animal mania trends has evolved, and certainly Valley animals and people are both better off for that knowledge. But if anyone has a notion of the next craze, let me know so I can get in early!

Bittersweet Racing

The 2020 Valley is not the racehorse breeding and training world it once was, and only a few establishments now work in this competitive and glamorous world. But the Valley had Thoroughbred glory days, and one man was at the top of the local racing scene.

Monty Roberts, now world renowned for his training methods and horseracing success, is perhaps our most famous animal person in the Valley. He has walls of buckles and trophies from competitive events, enjoys financial security from horseracing success, has authored horse and philosophy books, and regularly consults with the queen of England by way of advising her horseracing endeavors. He is constantly on travel demand, and not so much a presence in the Valley as in former years, and those early days certainly included some hard times and struggles.

Monty and his wife Pat's start-up days were far from easy street. In the late 1960s, when Monty and Pat took over Flag Is Up Farms from Hastings Harcourt, there were hardly ever adequate funds to meet the mortgage. The Thoroughbred racing world offers a difficult struggle with great rewards but also harsh financial realities that can lead to failure. However, it was a world Monty knew well, and he determined to soldier on to success.

In 1975, Monty made the trek to Keeneland in Lexington, Kentucky, the big-bucks Thoroughbred auction venue and center of the American racing world. He had a few thousand dollars as a budget plus some credit, and hoped to buy a winner. The idea was to purchase young horses with good potential, raise and train them in the Valley, and sell them down the line at a handsome profit. Sounds easy, but this world is full of broken hearts and empty bank accounts and, above all, much competition.

In the Keeneland pre-auction sale days, a colt caught Monty's eye, and he gave it a close inspection. There was something of a wounded deer about the animal, and Monty was fond of wounded deer. He inspected with his own theoretical measurements—hip bone to shoulder and center of scapula. (Don't try this at home!) The ragged young colt was not due to be expensive and looked poorly, but was bred to the teeth (by Hoist the Flag out of Premium Pout, winners both) and just seemed to have a look about him.

Monty is the original horse whisperer, and he probably spoke in the furry ear to say something like, "Son, you are bred for the track and look likely. Can you grow up and be a winner?" The young colt looked this cowboy in the eye and replied in a horsey way, "Boss, that sounds like a program!" The tense, bright-lights auction ring sale won the colt for Flag Is Up, and Monty spent forty thousand dollars (ten thousand down and thirty down the line) to bring the colt home.

The colt's arrival in the Valley, a staggering off of the fancy Thoroughbred van, was less than promising. He had lost weight, stumbled, and walked with his head hanging low. Monty's loyal, supporting partner Pat said she would never let him go to Keeneland alone again. His training partner, Crawford Hall, shook his head, and the stable hands looked away and got on with the job.

In the next months, the colt gained weight, was broke to ride, and began gracefully trotting and lightly cantering around the training track. However, the motion occasionally faltered, which the hopeful trainers explained as not really lameness, just a tendency to travel funny. There is a defect in Thoroughbreds to do with front-end nerve problems, much like lameness, that designates them as a "wobbler." Wobblers do not win races. Monty conferred with fellow trainers and vets, and the consensus came out: wobbler.

But Monty stuck with the colt who began to show improvement. When he ran, there was no wobble, and he did get on apace! An Irish trainer, Billy McDonald, visited to review potentials for the upcoming Santa Anita Park auction, and seemed to like the colt. Billy exclaimed, "Sure, and I have a feeling about that colt. I like his bloodlines and his way of going!" Flag Is Up Farms took heart and lavished every ounce of care, attention, training, and love on the young animal. There was much at stake. By chance, a Kentucky trainer, Hoss Inman, stopped by and told Monty the story of the colt's early background. Apparently, there had been a ruptured intestine, which caused a long operation, and the unconscious downtime had resulted in the poor condition and the wobbly trot that needed time for correction. The story got around with the news that Monty had something worthwhile.

Incredibly, the colt brought $175,000 at the Santa Anita Park sale. The mortgage was covered, and the Flag Is Up Farms reputation soared! All Monty's judgment was vindicated with a major, sale-topping success. Monty had a chance to buy back a share, but for once he quit while he was well ahead.

If that were the end of the story, all would be well, and our Valley hero would not wake up in the night pondering lost opportunities. But there is more.

The strong young horse was shipped to Ireland by new owner Robert Sangster and given a new name, Alleged. Monty had that opportunity to buy back a share, but he passed it up, the one decision he made about the horse that he came to regret. In Ireland, Alleged entered a race training program under the famous horseman Vincent O'Brien and began to show a strong potential. He won in Ireland, and then entered the big time in the European circuit.

The young horse won race after race, climbing the ladder of competition. Finally, he won the French Arc de Triomphe championship race, and then won it again a second year! Ultimately, the horse syndicated for breeding at sixteen million dollars! Monty's first judgment was completely correct, but the big prize had passed him by.

Valley travelers can drive by the Flag Is Up Farms track and stables on Highway 246 between Buellton and Solvang. While thinking about the racing drama that has gone on behind the gates, one can contemplate the cruelest blow of all. Vincent O'Brien was known to boast to his racing friends that he had bought the horse for a song from some cowboy in California who did not know what he had to offer!

Culture Clash

A few years ago, an incident demonstrated that there is not always peace among Valley animal people. A lady had bought ten acres on Alamo Pintado Road and submitted plans to the county that included establishing a kennel to house up to twenty Papillon dogs, producing at least six litters a year. Her ten-acre property might accommodate many times those small dogs' weight in cows or horses, and neighbors probably had dogs and cats well above any Papillon decibel and nuisance rate, but the neighbors unanimously bonded in opposition to the word kennel, and the fight played out in Santa Barbara County Planning Commission staff reports and hearing rooms.

The episode is instructive in defining our Valley evolution and our modern politics.

Papillons are small dogs (seven to ten pounds) with ancient lineage and large ears, which give them the name Papillon (butterfly in French). They are athletic, clever, lovable, and protective. Their owners and advocates describe them as "big dogs in little-dog suits." In the 1500s, renaissance artist Titian painted many of the aristocracy cuddling Papillons. Marie Antoinette is said to have walked up the executioner's scaffold steps (but, sadly, not down) carrying a Papillon, which defines them as the ultimate therapy dogs. But despite an ancient and famous lineage, these small dogs were newcomers in the panoply of Valley animals.

If the lady proposing the large family of small dogs had never indicated a kennel-type operation in her building permit application, she probably could have happily housed her pack, but the house blueprints submitted to the county included provisions for dog rooms and other facilities, which alerted the neighbors. Twenty horses would have gone unnoticed, but a perceived horde of exotic dogs inspired fear and loathing among the locals. Some land-use-experienced neighbors took on the threat, enlisting the agreement of virtually all the surrounding property owners, and the fight was on.

Each side enlisted savvy, personable, and respected Valley attorneys, Chip Wullbrandt for the property owner lady and Steve Kirby for the neighbors, and the land-use-permitting tussle began. The County Planning Commission staff turned out reams of paper and studies regarding noise levels, wastewater, legal precedence, agricultural use, neighborhood compatibility, California code, traffic, odor, and the sacrosanct California Environmental Quality Act. The sum of these studies duly submitted to the County Planning Commission was "ho hum, nothing to see here," and the use permit was granted. The neighbors recoiled and organized.

The next round of the dispute was to overturn the Planning Commission by appeal to the Board of Supervisors, and the neighborhood fight escalated. An impressive total of fourteen angry neighbor families is formidable opposition, and the supervisorial staff weighed in on the importance of these residents against a single nonvoting outsider. One anomaly also factored on the doubtful scale against the home/kennel proposer. She had stated that her plan was to give all the puppies produced by her home breeding facility away to new owners, and this seemed to defy logic in the kennel business. On the proposer's side were the facts that the county staff could not see any environmental, technical, or physical problem with this small-dog facility. The attorneys negotiated, the neighbors wrote letters, the lady fretted, and the supervisory hearing loomed. It became evident that in the county mind and decision-making scales, the Papillons were outsiders to Valley animal culture, and exotics were less than appealing to our country ways.

Finally, the embattled lady and her kennel home dreams became weary of the conflict. After all, who would want to be surrounded by actively angry neighbors? She called off the fight, and moved her plans to more favorable climates.

In some ways this was a win for the Valley, but also a sign of intolerance and a local lack of sympathy for an exotic, but sincere, animal lover. The property was to become a suitable and compatible home/ranchette, but in this episode, the Valley lost an interesting dimension.

· **F** ·

Presidential Pal

Doug Herthel was one of the characters who define the Valley and the relationship of locals to animals. He was a nationally known and gifted veterinarian who built the famous Alamo Pintado Equine Medical Center with many groundbreaking and inventive procedures. He treated Kentucky Derby horses with the same expertise and sympathy as a Valley kid's gymkhana pony. The clinic has a large practice in the Valley, and many horses owe their health and success to his innovative skills. He died in 2018, and the Valley and Valley animals miss him greatly.

One sunny day in the early 1980s, Doug and his wife, Sue, decided to drive out Jalama Road for a picnic. They noticed a horse trailer from the famous Cojo (pronounced KOH-hoh) Ranch passing them, and shortly thereafter Doug answered his cell phone to hear the ranch foreman's call for help with a horse in distress that was being driven to his Los Olivos clinic. Doug and Sue turned around to follow the trailer, and on arrival at the clinic found a severe colic case that needed treatment.

The Cojo is a major cattle operation with many horses and cowboys, and when the cow boss heard the bad news, he admitted that the ranch did not have a budget for this kind of horse treatment, and maybe it was best to put the horse down. Doug replied that the animal was too good for that, and the ranch response was to give the horse to Doug for whatever he wanted to do with it. Doug thanked him and operated, saving the lucky patient's life.

The horse mended, he became a member of the family, and Doug and his sons happily rode him around the Valley, discovering that the big bay gelding they now called Cojo had a splendid way of going, made a decent appearance, and seemed to be an all-around friendly soul.

Meanwhile, a famous rancher who lived in the hills above the Valley,

who also happened to be President of the United States Ronald Reagan, loved riding on his ranch, Rancho del Cielo. He enjoyed his simple ranch house and mountain spread more than the White House, his fancy residence in Bel Air, or any of the perks and trappings of the presidency. The Western White House did not have a big impact on the Valley, as the traffic came from the South and all the Valley tradespeople who serviced the ranch kept their silence.

Reagan's ranch kept a few horses for riding pleasure, and, seeking the best vet help around, his ranch manager would call on Doug from time to time. In the course of treating the Rancho del Cielo string, the president came to know Doug and, being the down-to-earth man he was, struck up a friendship with the veterinarian, and the two often visited about horse and ranching gossip. Doug also came to be good friends with the president's Secret Service chief of the ranch detail, John Barletta, and all the ranch staff.

In 1981, the president was given a very fancy and athletic white Arabian horse, named El Alamein, by President José López Portillo of Mexico.

The impressive animal was spirited, strong, independent minded, and a very questionable conveyance for a vacationing chief executive. President Reagan loved the horse, but his wife, Nancy; the ranch hands; the Secret Service; and all his staff trembled whenever the president insisted on riding El Alamein. Of course, unbeknownst to the president, his ranch people would ride the horse for hours to settle the spirited animal before the chief rode, and possibly even apply a mild horse sedative. But the big Arabian could still buck and skitter, and only the good horseman the president was could hope to stay on. Agent Barletta would ride security with a very reliable mount, Nancy would ride her happy horse called No Strings, and everyone watched anxiously as President Reagan mounted El Alamein for their ride around the ranch.

Finally, the ranch establishment, headed by Mrs. Nancy Reagan and Agent John Barletta, turned to Doug, demanding that he find a suitable and companionable horse for the president to befriend. Hopefully, a new horse friend would allow the feisty Arabian to enjoy a retirement to pasture, striking horse poses in the middle distance.

Meanwhile, the lowly cow horse, now known as Cojo, had thrived with lavish Herthel care, and with the special vitamin formula he administered, now known as Platinum Performance®. Cojo returned to full health, filled out to a good conformation, developed a shining bay sheen, and made friends with everyone in the clinic who clamored to ride him. Nothing seemed to faze the horse, and he had the best-possible disposition.

When the presidential ranch asked Doug to find a reliable horse, he replied that he had just the mount for the president.

On a beautiful California morning, happily refreshed by a good ranch sleep away from the cares of the office and nourished by a simple country breakfast, President Reagan emerged to go for a ride. On cue, the ranch staff, with Doug in attendance, presented the bad news that El Alamein had come up lame and could not be ridden, but there, in all his groomed and saddled glory, was our Cojo smiling at the commander-in-chief.

The president mounted and happily rode out with the First Lady and Agent Barletta to a brilliant canter around the ranch. As agreed, everyone exclaimed that, yes, it was a shame that the big white horse had gone lame, but wasn't this the best horse they had ever seen as a substitute?

The president agreed, and perhaps was even a little happy to have a new amiable horse friend instead of the problematical Arab skittering around the trail.

As time went on, President Reagan adopted the new, lucky horse as his best friend; renamed him Sergeant Murphy after a horse that featured in a film by that name; and merrily rode him over the hills. The ranch establishment thanked Doug and happily watched the boss bond with his new horse. Everyone heaved a sigh of relief seeing El Alamein doing what he did best, posing on the hillside.

President Reagan understood the horse had come as a gift from Doug, and thanked him profusely, but insisted that he pay for the horse, and of course his word prevailed. The president found a check somewhere and wrote out a payment to Doug for four thousand dollars, which he pressed into Doug's hand.

Now Doug had the problem of what to do with a payment he did not want, but finally decided to deposit the check because the president would know if he did not. Some days later, Doug received a call from the local bank manager who needed to speak with him. To everyone's consternation, the check was found to be invalid, with insufficient funds from the abandoned account. Needless to say, this was never mentioned to anyone, and the Herthel family still have a check signed by President Reagan marked insufficient funds.

When the president passed, Nancy Reagan told the ranch to give Sergeant Murphy back to Doug. The good horse carried Doug, Sue, and their sons, Mark and Troy, happily on Valley trails for a few years. He is now buried somewhere on the Reagans' Rancho del Cielo, and his headstone marks a truly exceptional, fortunate, and famous Valley animal.

· **F** ·

Pony Stars

Joel Baker lives on a hilly ranch just above McMurray Road in Buellton. Here he maintains one of the outstanding animal operations in the Valley, raising polo ponies. His day job is dispensing financial advice to clients from Los Angeles to Florida, but his true love and talent lies with polo. The athletic riders who play the game receive the adulation and publicity from their tournaments, but the real athletes and factors in winning a match are the all-important horses, the foundation for this amazing sport: the pony stars. Joel Baker has played polo most of his life and, in his successful career, learned early on that horses make and win the game.

As a young boy growing up in Los Angeles, across the street from the Will Rogers polo grounds, Joel came by his talents naturally while working as a groom and then part-time trainer for various high-rolling amateur polo players. In college, he majored in finance when he was not occupied in downhill ski racing, but he still maintained his passion and skills on the polo circuit. When he landed a thousand-dollar-a-month job working in downtown Los Angeles finance, he could hardly afford polo, but nevertheless, he worked out ways to play at Will Rogers field.

Most part-time, amateur players have a horse or two that give them problems on the field and become too rank for a hobby rider to handle. Joel would offer to take on those problem horses and apply his magic training skills until the horse settled down, behaved, and became playable again. His compensation for this training would then be the use of the horse for six months. On this basis, Joel promoted a competitive string of six sound, if somewhat unusual, playable horses to make up the necessary number and allow him to play in weekend tournaments.

In the early 1970s, a Hollywood Park racetrack trainer campaigned an exceptionally well-bred and talented mare called I'm Hep, a true "morning glory." Those aptly named horses produce extraordinarily fast times in the early-morning workouts but then, in the races, somehow fall apart and are unable to run well. At the starting gate, I'm Hep would break out in nervous lathers and fail miserably. The trainer knew Joel, and asked him to take the horse to the polo grounds, to see if a few normal months' work would help the failing attitude.

Joel worked with I'm Hep and, as they say, "got into her mind." He would give her long, quiet workouts and then, when polo match time came, saddle her quietly in the stable, away from the other horses, and canter out to play the first period before she had any time to think. In that six-minute opener of the match, she performed amazingly well, and even seemed to like playing the game. What she could not do on the track, she accomplished on the polo field. Joel's teammates wondered why he played so well early in the match and then seemed to fade riding lesser horses.

Joel finally gave the mare back to the trainer, but the complicated horse still would not produce on the track despite being, as they say, "bred to the teeth" and able to amaze the stopwatches in the early-morning workouts. The trainer and owner finally gave up and sold the horse to Joel for a few hundred dollars, paid out the best he could budget over a few months.

In 1981, Joel moved up to the Santa Ynez Valley and pursued a financial advisor and weekend polo career. To become better mounted, he starting a breeding and training program that included his new horse, renamed O-Wow because wow is what she felt like on the polo field. Her speed was beyond anything else, and she grew comfortable with turning, bumping, stopping, and all the demands of polo, which she took to naturally. She just seemed to like the game and know she was good at it! Joel started winning with her and became a valuable team player, starring in tournaments in California and around the country. Polo players are rated by so many "goals," with zero being a beginner and ten being the ultimate player, of whom there are few in the world. As Joel says, "This amazing mare took me to championships and a five-goal rating." Ultimately, Joel would be rated as a very impressive seven and a recognized international competitor.

Meanwhile, Joel's ranch kept turning out young polo ponies of exceptional talent, many of them descended from his spectacular O-Wow. These young colts and fillies do not necessarily want to be ridden by people, but with care, talent, and athletic ability, a rider can convince the horsey minds to accept a person on their backs, and Joel had the talent and perseverance to break and train the horses he bred. Of course, that is only the beginning of a polo pony's education, and running, stopping, turning fast, and bumping other horses, all the while chasing a little white ball with a half-crazed person on board, are all learned talents. A string of talented and competitive polo ponies is essential to the game, and Joel's ranch had a reputation for turning out horses that would make riders successful on the tournament fields. Generations of players from around the world have made the trip to our Valley to fill their string, and Joel still breeds, breaks, trains, and purveys doing what he loves.

But to continue with the story of his foundation mare, O-Wow, in addition to making him a world-recognized player in the 1970s, she established a line that has become famous. Her descendants are among the most prized ponies in the world. She passed on her speed and agility, but also that competitive Thoroughbred mindset that seems to make a horse want to play polo and get on with winning the game. And that is a rare quality prized and coveted by all serious polo players.

Consider taking a horse to a festive and nervous-making polo match venue, standing with a string of six horses waiting to be mounted, then prancing out onto a field with seven other nervous horses. Then, add chasing a white ball for six minutes hell-for-leather, running flat-out, stopping on a dime, and turning and running in the opposite direction, all alongside other horses that are straining to win the race or bump each other off the ball. After a few minutes of all-out effort, it is back on the line and stand quietly until home at last. This is well beyond most horses' ability and nature, but Joel's ranch turns out five to ten of these animals every year under Joel's training.

His foundation mare, O-Wow, bred to a local Thoroughbred, Cooper, and produced a colt, Santana, who in turn produced a stallion, Morning Star—all recognized as famous competitive horses. Morning Star bred to a mare, Empress, owned by Ken Berry, and produced a good-looking colt named Chocolatee. Ken played on this very talented horse for three years, until the horse was sold to a high-goal-team sponsor. One of the sponsor's professional players, perhaps the most talented ten-goal player in the world, Adolfo Cambiaso, played Chocolatee in Florida, and asked to take the horse to Argentina to play in the Argentine Open Polo Tournament. Here in this most famous championship, Chocolatee carried Cambiaso to victory and was voted "Best Pony" in two different years!

Joel reduced his breeding stock in 2018 from over two-dozen to around six, and limited his playing to nontournament, friendly games on weekends. But he still breaks and trains his young horses that can fetch from twenty to forty thousand dollars each. Of all the Valley animal sagas, his is one of unique talent and success.

Vintner Cats

In recent years, the Valley has become known for great wines and most enjoyable winery tours as publicized by the film Sideways. Wine fame is a function of climate, soil, and all the winemaking magic that has brought renown to our area over the years, but we should not ignore the Valley animals that have also contributed.

Wineries seem to be a magnet for mice. The large, sheltering buildings in a country setting, serving leftovers from workers' bag lunches and spills from fancy tour group repasts, serve to beckon creepy-crawlies in from the wild to the back recesses of the barrel rooms. But in addition to rodent droppings, nothing might put off a high-rolling buyer more than seeing a rodent scurrying across fermentation areas or dashing up a wooden upright tank. The constant war against winery rodents brings an enlistment and appreciation of exterminator cats into the winemaking process.

Mice invade not only wineries, but also brewhouses the world over. At the world-famous Glenturret Single-Malt Whisky distillery in Scotland, a bronze statue of a cat, Towser, standing with pride in the central courtyard, commemorates the animal that lived in the facility for twenty-four years from 1963 to 1987. During that time, the cat is claimed to have accounted for 28,899 mice! The beloved and much-missed cat is so memorialized as the ultimate enforcer in the Guinness World Records. What Towser and his mates did for Scotland many feline friends do for our Valley.

Vintners seek out resident cats who are brought to their winery homes by adoption, breeding, transfer from vintners' homes, and whatever

catnapping means a winery can devise. A good mouser is a prized member of the staff, and much sought after. Andrew Murray Vineyards was blessed for years with a loyal black tomcat named Curtis.

Curtis, so-called after the former name of the winery, arrived one day on his own time from no one knows where and was immediately adopted by the Murray facility he came to call home. Curtis was a feral cat, and completely independent, who came and went on his own whim. His very presence warned mice away, and when an unknowing rodent sought to take up residence in the winery, that critter was living on borrowed time. Sometimes the mood would come over the black tom to slink into the tasting room and work the visitors over for treats and petting, but mostly the cat came and went in private.

Curtis would sometimes ask for winery staff lunch treats and sometimes ignore any attempt at conversation. He was the soul of independence, but the Murray winery was his, and mice were the enemy. Finally, the black cat disappeared for reasons unknown. Cats deal constantly with enemy coyotes and mountain lions, or Curtis might have just taken up residence with a neighbor cat girlfriend. The Foxen Canyon neighborhood is populated with young cats that bear a resemblance to the famous Curtis.

Our Valley has many reasons for the success and fame of our wineries. Somewhere our Valley cats have earned their place on the list!

· 🅕 ·

Horse Matriculation

Friends from out of town have asked me about the Midland School and if this might be right for their children's education. My answer is always simple and straight to the point. If the student buys the unique program and ethos of the school, he or she will have the best high school experience imaginable. If the student does not like the program, he or she will and should leave the campus. Midland is very much a part of our Valley culture and tradition, and horses play a big part in the school life.

The Midland campus is a three-thousand-acre ranch on Figueroa Mountain Road up from Los Olivos and adjacent to the Los Padres National Forest. Founded in 1932, it has held true to its philosophy of individual development, intellectual curiosity and honesty, and a first-class education. School life is country and informal, and the emphasis is on character as well as intellect. The school is supported by an intensely loyal alumni. Knowing how to get along with a horse is a big part of the Midland experience.

About half the students, most of whom have never even known a horse previously, choose horseback riding for their athletic participation. New students who join the riding program begin with the basics of grooming, corral management, how to saddle and bridle, and generally how to get along with their new four-legged friends. As the students' Midland life progresses, they will work through four levels of horsemanship from the basics to lone trail riding, competitions including polocrosse, and even overnight campouts on neighboring ranches.

Some of the new students have never lived in the country and are amazed and delighted to be doing what they envisioned through TV

Western dramas. The challenge of horse management and riding becomes a very real factor in the young person's life, and personal responsibility is the name of the game.

The horses and all the tack and equipment have come through gifts to the school, mostly from Valley ranches and residents who understand and appreciate the Midland program. The quality of tack and equipment is readily apparent, but the value of a horse gift to the school requires a very savvy receiving judgment. It would be reasonable to suspect some horse owners might try to offload problem animals on the school, and the Midland staff need to be discerning. The twenty- to thirty-horse population has passed the experienced scrutiny for health, attitude, and suitability for young riders. The string, hanging out together in large paddocks or the more open pastures, have aced a test perhaps even more thorough than the one required for student acceptance to the school. In some cases, entering students are allowed to bring their own horse, and even show the animal in local competitions.

Midland is lucky to have Gina Butala, a young woman brought up on a California ranch, as the program manager. She is knowledgeable, sympathetic to students' ways, and no-nonsense in bringing young people into the Western world. She carefully coaches the students into four levels of participation and takes great pride when someone graduates to the fourth-level trail boss who can lead the new entries. When asked, she admits to no significant riding accidents outside of falls that have given serious bruises and damage to egos. She particularly enjoys the foreign students, many from Asia, who might never talk to a horse after Midland, but will hold a lifetime of treasured riding memories.

Midland also offers a trail riding program for local riders who might not have the opportunity to ride on a large spread. This is a great asset to a Valley filled with ten-acre horse ranchettes and a desire to explore the open spaces.

With ninety or so years of graduates from this unique Valley school, folks all over the world remember well their Valley high school days with special thoughts for their horse friends. The Midland string are a very special part of Valley life and animal culture.

Air Wars

El Rancho Marketplace is a splendid Valley-friendly market where locals meet each other while shopping—and where they, and their kids, probably worked for some time while growing up. Many take their morning coffee or lunch from the deli and sit at the tables outside to dine and watch their friends come and go. The food and coffee is delicious and fresh, but there is a problem: the local birds know this also, and take full advantage of any leftover scraps or simply steal customers' food from their plates.

This market institution is accustomed to the local animal population, and there is even a story about a young, confused coyote somehow dashing inside the market. The fact of this myth is attested to by the floor staff, but denied by the upstairs management. The birds, however, have become pests, and the clientele has complained.

Most of these birds are of the great-tailed grackle variety and, not being stupid, have learned to be aggressive in sharing people's food on the table. The annoyance to customers got real fast. The El Rancho management observed the bird invasion, understood the threat to retail food sales, and spent hours shooing the aggressive birds. But a standoff continued, and more birds learned about the free meals. The threat to diners' food and ambiance was beyond normal remedies, and became a drain on commerce. By good chance, the market's managers found a novel solution. If they could get a raptor-type bird, trained and on guard, their problems might go away.

A charming and friendly lady, Donna Sweet, somehow decided to share her life with birds of prey as a hobby and avocation. Her flying partner is a Harris's hawk named Grumpy, and the two work as a great team. These no-nonsense birds will attach themselves to a person in a partnership that may be hard for an onlooker to understand, but is meaningful and rewarding to bird people. When Donna is asked if training and bonding are difficult for bird and person, she simply states, "No, these birds just live by their stomachs." In other words, keep the sushi coming, and the hunter-killers will bond with you and do as you ask.

Raptor handlers are available for hire to sort out pesky bird problems. Their outstanding success locally is evidenced by the Tajiguas Landfill on the Gaviota Coast. Seagulls had invaded this facility in such force as to almost render the valuable Santa Barbara County asset inoperable, but a regular routine of hawks and handlers patrolling the facility has driven the gulls back to the ocean and saved the landfill. Donna occasionally fills in with Grumpy for this regular patrol gig.

When El Rancho found Donna, the grackle problem went away very quickly. The partnership is simple. Eight hours a week, bird and handler drive up from Goleta and hang out in the market parking lot. There are no set hours, but the ideal shift is morning coffee hour and midday lunchtime.

Grumpy the enforcer is all business when it comes to clearing birds out of a neighborhood. Donna patrols the property in a bright yellow parking attendant vest and wears a heavily gloved hand to serve as a hawk perch. She carries a pack loaded with raw meat for lure and reward, and can either work attached to Grumpy or allow him to fly free. His presence in the air will scatter panicked grackles, and he seldom needs to pluck them out of the air, but the food stealers know he can do that with ease if they remain in the neighborhood. When the birds see or sense his presence, they immediately head out for Solvang or Los Olivos, or even the Los Padres National Forest. With the patrol in regular attendance, they have learned to take El Rancho off their routes, and have also spread the bad news to their friends.

It is hard to know what goes on behind the earnest, beady hawk eyes. The fierce beak and claws command immediate respect, and that muscular flap of the wings indicates strength and agility beyond the few pounds of bird weight. A hawk can make short work of a mouse or squirrel that might wander by. People are safe, but still the threat is felt, and observers only hope that the intense glare of the hawk is not sizing them up for a meal.

Kate and I, out shopping, met Donna and Grumpy in the parking lot and enjoyed our conversation. Donna pointed out that, in speaking with her, we were ignoring the bird routine, and Grumpy was frustrated that we were not paying attention to him. Finally, he flew down to the ground from Donna's wrist and "chicken walked" to inspect some bushes. We learned that this was his way of turning his back on us and indicating that if we were not paying attention to him, he would just ignore us also. I was surprised to see such perception and personality from an otherwise-airborne hunter-killer.

The bird is beautiful and purposeful, and it was an amazing experience to observe a wild creature bonding with a person and performing a useful task on request. One day on duty, Donna counted over fifty birds that scattered and vacated after one swoop and wing spread from Grumpy. It seems that eight hours a week at different times of day will do the job. The word must go out somehow in bird world that a crust of sandwich snatched from the El Rancho lunch table is not worth the very real possibility of being struck from the sky by the enforcer. We watched as two odd, inquisitive birds perched on some phone wires eyeing the tables. On a signal from Donna, the hawk sped into the air and spread his feathers at the birds, braking his speed and displaying his might. The birds were long gone by the time Grumpy, hearing Donna's whistle, sped back for his sushi reward.

A Valley bonus is that Donna very much enjoys her job because of the interest and friendship from the local customers shopping at El Rancho. The market solved a problem and, in doing so, gained a handsome bird attraction.

Trolley Tradition

The "Ding! Ding!" of the Solvang trolley perpetuates a Danish tradition of the good life. Beginning in the early 1900s, Copenhagen dwellers dressed in their best, boarded trollies to ride through town, and most likely headed for the famous Tivoli Gardens, to enjoy an outing. Lingering over a glass of Carlsberg beer, listening to the Tivoli bands, watching the passing scene on long Scandinavian evenings, and then riding the trolley home is bred into the Danish community of Solvang. And the tradition is alive and well in our town today, though threatened by the current coronavirus shutdowns.

In 1979, Hans Rasmussen secured a replica of the Danish trolley and initiated Solvang tours. Locals and tourists could buy a ticket to ride the sometimes-motorized and sometimes-horse-drawn vehicle through town and dream of Copenhagen nights. Over the years, the trolley franchise went through many stages of ownership and style, and as of this writing, it has landed on a friendly and talented horse-savvy family with a splendid pack of Percheron breed horses.

Sal Orona is one of those individuals in the tradition of the "Horse Whisperer" with a rare talent to train and befriend horses. After immigrating from Mexico a generation ago, he worked in various horse-training capacities, and finally in 2007 acquired the Solvang trolley and permit to operate the well-known tourist attraction. His family also operates the Solvang Trolley Ice Cream Parlor where those waiting to ride can enjoy the best ice cream waffle cone they will ever have in their lives. While Sal provides the horse-driving talent, his daughter, Claudia, provides the personality as tour conductor and guide for tourists from

Asia, Europe, and all over the United States.

Sal will rise early on his ranch on the San Lorenzo Seminary road, feed his string of eight to twelve Percherons, and choose his team for the day. As of this writing, he can match up four different teams of a Percheron pair, selected for the workday by the horses' mood and Sal's instinct. Next comes the cleanup of the big horses and harness, and loading in the trailer. The twenty-minute ride to Solvang brings him to a lot where the trolley is stored for unloading horses and harnessing them to the trolley. With a quick change into his own driving costume, he is ready for his first tour.

The horses are all flax-colored great Percherons. The leading harness horse in the Americas before the age of motors nudged them off the road, these large and friendly animals are bred for pulling heavy loads and pleasant disposition and, among the many horse breeds, known for their desire to do the right thing . . . perfect for tourist work. The Orona family built up their string from some purchases, but also from gifting of surplus or problem horses who would otherwise become orphans. Sal had built a reputation for his ability to train the big animals that might in another situation have presented problems. He just had that "Horse Whisperer" knack, and anyone who can convince a big Percheron to negotiate Solvang traffic for a day while pulling a trolley full of noisy tourists certainly has a rare skill.

The trollies can handle up to twenty riders who have bought a ticket for a modest fourteen dollars. The tour will wind through Solvang streets as Sal negotiates traffic and pedestrians while Claudia manages the passengers and explains the sights and history of Solvang. It is truly a "slow down and see the world" experience that can make a day in our town perfect.

Traffic is always a problem, and driver and horses need to think alike and be very aware of impatient tourist. Sal swears that some of his horses respond to a red light change by stopping, but that sounds like a Hans Christian Andersen fable. In his years of operation, there has only been one accident, when a drunk driver rear-ended the trolley. Locals know that they might be slowed down by the rig, but are usually forgiving. Visitors are just amazed to see a vestige of the old world making its horse and trolley way. Valley residents more often than not have never taken a ride, but they are making a big mistake not to enjoy the experience. They are missing a learning and fun opportunity, and horse and trolley slow motion is good for the soul.

As of this writing, in the pandemic times of 2020, the trolley service has been discontinued. As the coronavirus spread its way through our county, Solvang tourist businesses shut down completely, and the gradual reopening has not included the trolley. City Hall was forced to cancel the permit for the quarantine duration, and there are even rumors that the town streets, some of which have been closed to traffic, may no longer accommodate the slow-moving symbol of a past age. If that is the case, and the trolley franchise is disallowed, Solvang will have lost a part of its heritage and unique nature.

The noble and willing Percherons have given our town a unique window into Solvang's Danish history and culture. If, somehow, our horse-drawn trolley tours are not permitted to resume, a warm and unique people–animal scene of the Valley will have sadly come to an end.

Part Three

RANCH WORK

Thundering Hooves

The winding Ballard Canyon Road is a stellar country vista in the Valley, a must for bicycle trekkers and wandering drivers. The ranches in this area, a favorite stomping ground for many Valley animals, seem frozen in time. In 1999, the Larry Saarloos family bought the Windmill Ranch that stretches along a good part of the canyon, and received a bonus with their purchase.

The Saarloos family, with a pure Dutch history, grew up in Southern California on a dairy farm. When the dairy sold, and after a number of successful ventures, the Saarloos gang moved to the Valley. Larry was more content on a tractor than with any hint of retirement, and his farming background led him to cattle ranching, grapes, and a winery that produces excellent Santa Ynez Valley wine. Larry's son, Keith, once did the DNA testing thing, and the results came back 99.6 percent Dutch heritage. The family has worried about the 0.4 percent ever since.

When escrow closed on the new ranch, the former owner threw into the deal a herd of thirty-five buffalo that made their home on the ranch. Larry wondered at the generosity, and what the former owner knew about buffalo that a dairyman did not, but accepted the offer graciously. This began a sympathetic, but sometimes adventuresome, twenty years of Saarloos–buffalo relationship.

Buffalo, with 1,500-plus pounds and two mean horns, have no enemies, and maintain a somewhat somnolent and benign attitude toward life unless riled. They can evidence a playful nature, and were happy with the abundant grass and hills on the Windmill Ranch. The ranch was surrounded with enhanced fencing, with sturdy fence posts only five feet apart, a good four feet high, and strung with six cross strands of barbwire, a barrier much stronger than the usual cattle fence.

Once Larry spotted a tourist carload reaching through the fence to try to entice some buffalo with a peanut butter sandwich, or something. Larry told them to back off, and that the fence was more for keeping people out than for keeping the buffalo in—if the herd wanted to move, the fence would be so much brushwood.

The herd mated regularly and produced calves that prospered, but unlike cattle would never be rustled or mixed with other herds, and so were never branded. Roping them might be a problem too. The ranch sold the occasional buffalo to other ranches or exotic food fare companies. The Saarloos family occasionally enjoyed the lean and tasty meat, well marinated and barbecued, but like good ranchers, they very much preferred beef. Additionally, cutting horse trainers would buy the occasional animal for training purposes. Apparently, a buffalo will act very much like a steer in the cutting arena, and keep up the game far longer, perfectly suited to horse training. The only problem with these occasional transactions was with loading the animals in a trailer for transportation to the buyers. Putting a buffalo down a chute and into a trailer is more than a little Western, and makes a circus train loading look like child's play.

The Saarloos family lived happily on the ranch with the herd, and enjoyed showing off the animals, not to mention the fascination of tourists stopping on the road to view the exotic creatures. Bicyclists regularly paused to gape, and once Larry noted that Lance Armstrong, leading the training pack of international U.S. Postal Service Pro Cycling Team competitors, brought the entourage to a halt to enjoy buffalo watching.

The buffalo years did bring the occasional challenge. Once Larry was riding with Keith when they passed by the herd. The buffalo, with a more playful than threatening attitude, began to trot along with the two. Horses are deeply suspicious of buffalo, and the two mounts became increasingly nervous in the loose company. When a horse rolls its eyes, it is time to pay attention. Finally, Keith's horse turned abruptly, throwing the saddle sideways, and Keith landed on the ground. With a few horned 1,500-pounders trotting behind, complete with loud chuffs, Keith did not wonder for a second if they only meant to play, and set a new record across country. Keith is not made to be a sprinter, and high-hurdling the fence was not in the cards either. But he found that reserve of speed hidden away in all of us when the alternative is disaster. He made it to the fence in record time and slid under with only a few barbwire scratches. He never knew if the buffalo objective was gore or snuffle, but he had no intention to find this out.

Finally, in 2019, Larry sold the last of his herd. He and the family miss the strange beasts and the occasional sound of running hooves. In losing the buffalo, the Valley lost a fascinating attraction and a rare dimension of our Valley animals.

Recently the Valley has also lost Larry Saarloos and is greatly diminished by his passing, although his persona and family live on as a strong presence.

Roundup

All of the stories in this book are based on facts and true incidents; however, this episode combines a number of actual ranching moments to describe one possible present-day roundup. While their names have been omitted by request, this ranch story tells of our current variation of Spanish dons, Mexican vaqueros, generations of hardworking cowboys, and the modern, more gentrified ranchers who maintain the less spacious properties encircling the Valley.

Mr. and Mrs. Owner lived on a medium-sized (two-thousand-acre) cattle ranch in the surrounding hills, and had many friends with similar operations. On this occasion, they had invited Mr. and Mrs. Guest, among others, to the family ranch to help gather four hundred steers from a fifteen-hundred-acre pasture—a necessary working day combined with a pleasant social outing.

When the Valley turns from green to gold, the grass on the ranches has been mostly eaten by the cattle, and steers need to be gathered from the eaten-down hills and shipped by truck to lush northern pastures. This was such a day.

Before daylight, the Guests woke up and loaded their two horses into a truck and trailer. The horses were provided with hay bundles to munch on while the couple drove to seek their early breakfast at Ellen's Danish

Pancake House in Buellton with coffee and, of course, pancakes. Years ago, the gathering eatery might have been the Solvang Restaurant, but in the current era, this establishment had pretty much been taken over by tourists. Ellen's provided early cheer, friendly waitresses, and a few fellow ranchers headed in the same direction.

A half-hour before departure time, the Guests parked in the Owners' ranch barnyard, unloaded, saddled and bridled, and greeted the host, local cowboys, and friends similarly preparing. While the host ranch foreman was the most experienced hand, he knowingly deferred to the ranch owner as this was both a working and a social day and, as long as the task got done, part of his job was to let Mr. Owner be the cow boss. The Owners offered coffee and Danish to those who had not pancaked, and some made an effort at early-morning humor. Mrs. Guest held their two horses while her husband made that all-important stop behind the trailer to unload coffee before the long ride.

Close to the appointed time, some twenty riders mounted and headed off into the hills in the dawn light. The group had a good forty-five-minute ride uphill to the back of the ranch. It was a beautiful Valley morning, with mist gradually clearing in the heat of the rising sun, and the smell of horses, cattle, oaks, and grass wafting in the cold Valley air.

Finally, the group stopped at the back fence, high on a hilltop. By now, the sun was up, but still a chill hung in the air. With the cattle feeding in the open rather than hunkered down in the shade of the oaks, the easy-friendly riders were looking forward to the familiar task, and formed a circle to receive assignments and any instructions.

The ranch foreman deferred to Mr. Owner to assign areas of gathering responsibility. The Guest couple were assigned a hilly, wooded section that bordered the large pasture with a barbwire fence. They knew it would be a long up-and-down ride, likely not heavily populated with steers, and relatively easy to gather because of the fence, but problematical with the rises and falls of the hills and valleys. A local cowboy on a doubtful young horse was assigned to ride the section with them. When the riders split up to find and drive their own assigned portions of the ranch pasture, soon the Guests and their cowboy found themselves on their own in the quiet hills, and headed to the far corner of the ranch to begin their sweep.

After a few minutes of riding their section, they encountered a dozen steers in a clearing and fanned out to push them in the direction of the distant corrals. The cattle seemed to accept the game, and walked along willingly in front of the three horses. From time to time, one of the riders slapped a thigh or made a noise to keep progress in the steers' wooly minds, but the animals were agreeable and carried on in the right direction. As time and the ride went on, across the grassy clearings and over the oaky hillsides, more steers joined the small herd in front of the three. The walking progress continued apace, with an occasional steer gallop downhill and trot back up the other side. The cowboy had the occasional wrestle with his young horse, but knew his job, and Mr. and Mrs. Guest were experienced at this business. The steers meandered ahead of the horsemen in a bovine way, and all was productive and picturesque.

Either people have a cow sense, or they do not. The ability to think like a steer is a highly prized and necessary instinct in cowboys and ranchers. Some seem to be able to read a cow's mind and know which way it will go, and whether it will duck out or otherwise do the wrong thing, and to react in time with their horse to make sure it does not stray. If a professional cowboy is without this instinct, he might as well seek another line of work. Mr. Guest, despite his city-business background, had been around cattle enough, and somehow possessed the cow-sense instinct to be effective in herding cattle.

By now, there were some fifty steers in the herd in front of the three. The bunch were approaching the top of a rise, and something transmitted itself from one of the lead steers to Mr. Guest. Whether it was a turn of the head, a rolling of the eye, a backward glance, or just a step out of rhythm, this steer showed a mind to run backward down the hill, possibly taking a portion of the herd along. Mr. Guest applied a spur, and his horse reacted instantly. When the steer did turn the wrong way, he was immediately blocked by horse and rider who emitted a sharp "Yeah!," causing the steer to change course and trot off in the right direction with the herd.

Moments like this make a successful roundup or a fiasco. Even the best rider can make a mistake, and a determined cow can run right through horse and rider if it has a mind to. The skill is to prevent such a disaster before it happens. Most of the riders that day had witnessed when a green hand rode into a nervous bunch of cattle about to be driven through the corral gate and then made an uncalled-for noise found only in Western movies. The herd stampeded in an explosion of animals back into the hills, only to be retrieved with much time and trouble. This is the kind of moment that can never be lived down and will be talked about for generations.

On this day, Mr. Guest made a good move, saved some time and trouble that would have occurred had the steer broken out, and absolutely did the right thing. His wife took satisfaction, and the cowboy just thought it was all in a day's work.

After about two hours of riding, the four hundred steers were assembled in the field leading to the corrals. Now another call for skill came into play as the herd was filtered into the corral gate. Some animals might not have wanted to go, and some might have wanted a return to the hills. The twenty riders had to push just enough, but not too much to spook the herd, and be very alert to any steer making a bolt from the others. The ranch foreman was very much front and center, controlling this movement. This morning, as not always in current Valley ranching life, the task was accomplished with a minimum of confusion. The herd made it to the corrals, to pass the time peacefully before the cattle-shipping trucks showed up, and the riders' gathering work was done.

Two different riders took the responsibility of counting the steers into the corrals. Amazingly, the two counts came out the same, and their totals confirmed that the gathering was a success, the herd all accounted for. This does not always happen, but comes out right most times. With the long ride and work accomplished, the twenty rode back to the barns and trailers, happy, tired, and hungry.

The first reward was an iced tub of beer. The Valley has struck gold both in wine and in crafted beer, and the cold, brilliantly made liquid went down happily and gratefully while the crew unsaddled and tied their horses to trailers in the back of the barn.

Custom next dictated the host ranch provide a barbecue feed. The proud Owners had gone to some trouble to lay out a spread, highlighted by tri-tip steaks on the grill. As this event was in the Valley, a selection of delectable local wines, then a full feast with all the fixings, were offered. It was also tradition that the guests bring dessert, and the Guest couple had sprung for a Solvang bakery special that would suit the queen of Denmark.

The hungry, happy group of friends who had just accomplished an appetite-inducing piece of work assembled at trestle tables. The ranch owner types drifted to one set of tables, and the foreman and hands drifted to other tables, but there was an air of conviviality, bolstered by good food and good wine. The barbecue morphed into a wine and pastry gossip and joke session interspersed with old stories and banter. The foreman and hands drifted off to accomplish the more mundane chores such as putting up the boss's horse and hauling hay bales to feed the steers before the cattle trucks arrived. Soon a few old Valley ranching friends were left happily passing time sipping wine and telling lies.

At last the sun began to dip, and an afternoon chill set in. By this time, most of the visiting riders had departed, but a few still sat around spinning yarns and enjoying the moment. Finally, Mrs. Guest whispered that it was time to go, and her husband gulped the last of his splendid red wine, stumbling a little as he got up and walked back to the horse trailer.

When they rounded the barn, they discovered that their horses and trailer had vanished. Some confusion and alarm ensued, but was tactfully dispelled.

Just then, the foreman pulled up, driving the host family pickup. "Sir, the boys returned your horse and rig," he said, "and I would be happy to give you a lift home."

A good foreman has a cow sense and also a people sense. All the herding was well done that day.

Trail Combat

Wild-animal encounters are famous in wild-bear Alaska, lion-stalking Africa, or hungry-tiger India, but incidents of the wild meeting the domestic also occur in the Valley. One recent day a local innocent horseback ride almost ended in tragedy.

The Walker family live on the hilly side of Ballard Canyon, where homesteads blend into the open country across Highway 101 and into

the hills beyond. Many critters walk these hills, including stealthy, hungry coyotes.

The Walker home housed teenage daughters, as well as a large Rhodesian Ridgeback, eighteen months old at the time of the famous coyote incident. A chance encounter during an otherwise pleasant trail ride brought out the mighty heritage of this otherwise happy, homebody dog.

Rhodesian Ridgebacks descend from a heroic history of lion hunting during their early days of evolution on the African outback. With shades of athletes and killers lingering in their distant past, the kindly, large dogs are family friendly and obedient rug loungers in the modern world. Those who own Ridgebacks love them for their playful, open personalities, and many families make their homes with a benign and loyal brown dog friend, complete with a distinct dark ridge down its back.

One sunny day, a young Ella Walker, with her sister Georgina, set out for a trail ride with Khula the Ridgeback happily trotting along in the lead and a very small rescue dog of mixed heritage, named Cadbury, perched on the front of Ella's saddle. About a half-mile from home, but still well out on a neighbor's ranch, Ella let the small dog down to trot along behind the two horses, with the Ridgeback still in the lead. It was a very benign and happy Valley scene, with two teenage girls on easy horses, accompanied by two dog friends.

Suddenly, out of nowhere, a coyote appeared, dashing straight for Caddy. They clashed, with the coyote rolling over the small dog dinner and standing over the terrified Caddy, about to tear the small critter to shreds. But just as fast, the Rhodesian woke up, spun, and sprinted back to knock the coyote off little Caddy and roll it over in the dirt.

All three stood up for an instant of indecision and astonishment. The African heritage awoke and drummed in Khula's brain. The small Caddy shrank in terror. The coyote stood—thinking he was in charge, still hungry, looking at dinner—and then made a terrible mistake.

The coyote lunged to take back the small dog, but the Rhodesian grabbed the menace by the head and shook the startled coyote away, tearing off an ear in the process. The coyote hit the ground running as fast as only a motivated wild animal can run, with Khula in hot pursuit. The two disappeared into the hillside brush.

Later, back at the stable, with horses unsaddled and turned out, a still-shaking Cadbury lay cradled in Ella's lap. Khula turned up shortly from around the barn, looking proud and totally ready to accept praise and affection from two grateful girls and a shaken but unmarked housemate. The coyote may have survived, but was never seen again.

Volunteer Firemen

The Valley lives with the knowledge of brush fire potential, and that possibility struck for real on Dennis R. Patrick's Zaca Creek Ranch, north of Buellton, in September 2019. Apparently, some careless vehicle had caused sparks to fly off Highway 101, and three separate locations caught fire late in the afternoon. Firefighters and equipment arrived quickly, but wind fanned the flames, and the three blazes spread wildly through the dry grass and brush. By nightfall, thanks to three planes, four helicopters, and over a hundred firefighters, the flames were contained.

The ranch had a population of about sixty cows and calves, and while they normally stay well out of the way of a fire, there is always the possibility of finding themselves trapped in a canyon or, particularly with young calves in the herd, making a wrong turn and not outrunning the flames. A Santa Barbara County firefighters' legend comes from a fire a few years ago when a herd of around fifty deer had somehow lost their bearings, panicked, and burned to death surrounded by a fast-moving wildfire.

A local cowboy, John Solem, had the lease on the Zaca Creek Ranch, and the sixty-cow-and-calf herd was a significant investment for him. He dashed to the ranch, with his cow horse in a trailer, to move his cattle, but, of course, a single cowboy could never do the job alone.

Around the Valley, when the smoke was spotted and the news broadcast the location of the brush fire, ranchers and cowboys automatically took note, and the cattle-savvy friends of John Solem sprang into action. In short order, a dozen cowboys with horses and trailers arrived at the ranch ready to help in any way. Normally, the sheriffs and firemen seal off approach roads and ranch entrances to wildfires, but they know the problems with ranch cattle herds and fires, and directed the cowboy help to parking and probable herd location. The firemen had also cut a number of fences to let in firefighting dozers and trucks, which might have let the cattle out on Highway 101, so they wanted the loose cattle herded away from the busy road.

Within minutes, the volunteers mounted, found the herd, fanned out into "round 'em up and move 'em out" formation, and headed them into a holding pen. It was soon determined that the pen might be in the dangerous path of the spreading flames, so the herd was next moved off the ranch, through an opening quickly cut in the wire fence, and onto the adjoining Jonata Vineyard. Here were welcoming holding pens to keep the herd safe. And that is how ranchers and cowboys operate for mutual aid in the Valley.

Meanwhile, across the freeway, heavy equipment operator Ben Johnson saw the action, knew the ranch well from previous work, and recognized that he might be needed. Sure enough, when he chugged his dozer up toward the ranch headquarters, he saw that a valuable generator, fueled by a large propane tank, might be caught up in the blaze and needed a protective shield dozed immediately. He began ploughing up circles around tank and generator, only to be harassed by a low-flying Sheriff's Department helicopter broadcasting instructions to clear the area. Ben, who knew what he was doing and where he was relative to the fire, had no intention of surrendering the valuable tank and generator of his friend, ranch owner Dennis. Ben replied to the broadcast move-on instructions from the hovering helicopter by extending his arm with a hand signal indicating a rude but definite international sign of no thanks. He continued his dozer blade circling and saved the equipment.

Ben had a couple more interesting scenes with the fire. While moving his dozer, he came on a family of fox, a very unusual sight in coyote- and lion-dominated country. They seemed to be circling in confusion, but on seeing the dozer, the fox family fled, thankfully, in a safe direction. He also saw the big boar that hangs out on the ranch, who has come to be known as Frank, walking with dignity—not even trotting—away from the approaching flames. Later, just to be helpful, he followed the herd movement on his four-wheel truck. A young calf, as they sometimes do, had become exhausted when the herd was driven, and decided to give up and lie down. Ben stopped, picked up the little animal, and drove her to join the herd in the corral, and rewardingly saw the baby calf join up with her mother cow.

The next day, only spots of smoldering oak tree flames remained, and with the exception of ground squirrels, disgruntled quail, and miscellaneous destroyed nests, all animal life returned to normal.

· **F** ·

Family Way

The Valley was very sad with the passing of Dr. Doug Herthel, the founder, with his wife Sue, of the Alamo Pintado Equine Medical Center in 1972. Luckily for the locals, the Herthels' son, Troy, a capable veterinarian who worked closely with his father, is very much carrying on the skills and Herthel presence in the clinic—a relief for Valley horses also. Vets are important to the Valley scene, both for their expertise and for their diplomacy and sensitivity.

A familiar client once told Dr. Troy he had acquired an important new family member, a well-bred and talented pony that he had purchased for his children from a farm in Texas. The little mare, brought to Troy for a checkup, was found to be healthy and appealing in all respects. Now named Strawberry, she had looks, personality, and a seeming inclination to do the right thing in every pony way.

After a few weeks, however, the client noticed that the pony seemed to be gaining weight, most likely because the daughters were feeding the greedy little gal Danish pastry and many other treats that ponies crave. But even with bootleg food banned and a strict feeding regime, the small horse seemed to grow fatter and fatter. Finally, the client became worried about the overall health of the animal, and brought her to Troy to check into the problem.

Following a complete examination and ultrasound, Troy hesitatingly informed the client that the pony was no maiden, but very much in a family way. "Impossible!" the grandfather-to-be replied. "There has been no stallion with her, and no notice of breeding with the sale!" Troy repeated that there was no question of the condition and congratulated the growing family.

When the man contacted the ranch in Texas, he was met with a complete and indignant denial that such a breeding could have occurred. Strawberry wasn't confessing, so the mystery continued as the little horse expanded.

Finally, the day came, and Troy responded to a panicked call from the family—one of the daughters, albeit a horsey one, was about to give birth!

While the delivery went smoothly, the outcome was a bit of a surprise. The small miracle was healthy, but proudly displayed the two unmistakably large ears of a baby mule! As Strawberry gazed upon him with pride and love, the family stood agape with astonishment and wonder.

Troy offered to supply the names of mule breeders and purveyors in order to move the newborn on as soon as possible, but the little mule rapidly made himself a home, was named Shortcake, and prospered with his loving pony mom and welcoming family. It did not take long for Shortcake to learn the girls were a source of treats, especially Danish pastry; the mom was a well of supplemental milk bottle feeding; and the dad a hand that would scratch his back and behind his big ears any day.

Troy could only figure that a romantic Texas donkey had somehow slipped through a fence for a romantic, moonlight pasture breeding, totally unknown to the ranch or pony suppliers. Mules are the product of donkey stallions and horse or pony mares and develop abilities and personalities quite apart from and often beyond horses. Shortcake went on knowing he would be bigger and smarter than his mother, and beloved by the host family, but one chromosome short of being able to reproduce.

Unwanted Boarders

Valley residents share the hills with a large population of wild boar. These shy and potentially ferocious animals lurk about in small herds, sometimes providing barbeque fodder for locals, but also the occasional hair-raising encounter.

A couple of Valley characters, Carlyle Eubank and veterinarian Chris Pankau, were riding on the Bar Go Ranch in the hills above Happy Canyon when they came across a herd of wild boar meandering over a meadow. They were both handy amateur ropers, and on Chris's dare, Carlyle ran down a medium-sized pig, just as he would chase a young calf. For once in his life, he threw a perfect loop and caught the boar square around the neck, and as a normal reaction pulled the rope tight, closing the noose.

Now as they rushed headlong for the brush, he had some quick survival thinking to accomplish.

The next normal calf-roping action would be to dally the rope around the saddle horn and rein in horse and calf to a sudden stop. His horse was trained to do that, and also stand still while the rider dismounted and ran down the rope to throw down the calf, tie its legs to immobility, and then do whatever doctoring was necessary, or at least unloose and retrieve the rope. Meanwhile, the horse would obediently wait, but maybe not in this case for a scrambling wild boar. With a 150-pound angry pig armed with lethal tusks, a normal calf-roping routine was out of the question.

Now with boar leading the charge, affixed to galloping horse and rider by a taut rope, the pig refuge brush-covered sidehill was rapidly approaching. Carlyle's horse might run ahead of the boar to let him loosen the noose, but then the boar might slash the horse's legs. In no way did Carlyle want to stop the boar. In a split second, he did the inevitable. He cast the rope to the wind, and boar and rope vanished a hundred miles an hour into the brush.

Chris rode up behind Carlyle and drawled, "That was pretty Western, but how come you let 'im get away?" With no reply, the sweaty horse and rider contemplated buying and breaking in a new rope on the slow walk back to the barn.

European wild boar were imported and introduced into Monterey County for hunting purposes by ranchers in the 1920s. After the cold winters and dangerous Black Forest wolf conditions, the boar thought they had gone to heaven and thrived in California. Meanwhile, domestic pigs often escaped from ranches, and set up in a family way with these new wild cousins. The result today is a thriving population of semi-wild boar.

These animals tear up the oak sidehills for acorns, and dine off any crop they can find along the way. Ranchers are not generous with their own livelihood and often shoot boars on sight, as well as offer hunts for profit. There are rare stories of boars treeing hikers or farmers, and they can be dangerous, but mostly remain shy of people and anxious to keep out of the way.

In the 2000s, Dennis R. Patrick purchased a large hilly ranch just off

Highway 101. He intended to raise cattle and live a peaceful country life in the Valley, and did not know he shared that vision with a healthy boar population. One day he was out walking and stood amazed as a dozen huge boar meandered on a nearby hillside, followed by a host of baby piglets.

Dennis hired a young headstrong cowboy who had previously hunted boar for sport, but soon learned better. Once, on the trail of a boar, the animal charged and knocked him flat, but fortunately he retained hold of his rifle. Lucky for his cowboy legs, he was wearing a pair of heavy chaps, which the hulking black pig ripped apart with his tusk as he galloped over and beyond. The cowboy kept his cool and, when the boar turned for a second pass, shot him with a heavy .44 rifle. The chaps still hang in the ranch tack room as a warning to future aggressive ranch hands.

Another day, Dennis's ranch manager was walking his horse down a narrow trail when three young boar startlingly bolted toward him, then around the horse, disappearing behind. The rider had a split moment to ponder this unusual sight, when he looked again and saw a mountain lion dashing after the pigs, pursuing its lunch. Horse, rider, and lion froze, with the lion stopping and looking.

The rider could not handily turn and run, but there is a horse defense that, though rarely experienced, can be effective. Horses have the capacity to blow a loud, windy snort when challenged, and in this standoff, the manager's horse emitted a startling and colossal snort/chuff that totally impressed the lion. The huge cat bounded off the trail and vanished down the sidehill, leaving the rider with all bodily juices drained into paralyzing adrenaline, not to be restored until later—after making salubrious inroads into a six-pack back at the barn.

Dennis admits he took leave of his senses one day by suggesting to his ranch manager that it might be interesting to capture and raise a young boar on the ranch to see how it behaved. His loyal manager took this to heart and soon had an opportunity to make good on the request.

While driving the tractor with some chore in mind, he came upon a group of small piglets running about in the grass. He stopped, dismounted, and grabbed one. The idea was to pen this specimen and raise it in domestic bliss. The baby boar was tractable and easily carried but, with a historic pair of lungs, emitted a squeal that shook the oak trees. Sure enough, big fat mama boar, alarmed and very angry, emerged from the brush to save her baby and, incidentally, leave a kidnapper in tatters.

He broke sprinting records to dash back to the tractor with monster mama in close pursuit. Momentarily, the scene resolved with the driver standing on the tractor seat but unable to start up the tractor, looking down at the slathering, trotter-pawing, tusk-chomping boar power, unable to climb aboard. The lively impasse continued until it finally dawned on the stand-up piglet napper that he had the squealing baby still under his arm! He gently tossed the baby back to mother care, and the two trotted happily back into the bush.

As the sweating manager climbed back onto the tractor seat, he swears the huge mama boar looked back at him as if to say, "No more games!" He was happy to agree.

Cattle Love

This episode happened a few years ago, but still says much about our Valley and Valley characters.

Jack Grimes had retired from Southern California contracting, bought a small ranch, moved in some cattle, and took strongly to cowboy ways. Rudy Eisler, also semi-retired from Southern California real estate success, had bought a neighboring property, moved in some heifers, and taken up a ranching mode. Neither knew a great deal about country-type farming operations, but with a little help from their friends, both settled in nicely with their respective cattle happily munching in benign peace, eyeing each other across the barbwire. The neighbors were friends and enjoyed Valley life in small-acreage ranching harmony.

One day, Jack mentioned to Rudy that his heifers seemed happy, but would do a great deal better if a bull was introduced into their home life. A few calves might even result that would be a bonus. He had an extra bull, and would be happy to give it to Rudy to complete his ranch scene. This seemed like a logical and good idea, and soon the young bull was brought next door to meet the heifers. Locals with cattle experience had wondered about Jack's bull, but let him get on with his breeding program.

Both Jack and Rudy came and went regularly, and the cattle were left to get on with life while the ranches were left to the care of some temporary hired help. Jack had not been threatened by the bull, but a couple of times being snuffled at a distance had given him doubts.

A couple of days after the cattle exchange, Rudy returned to hear with alarm from his hired hand that the bull had torn up the water line, destroyed a trough, and eliminated a few sections of fence to return to his former home and the cows he loved. Contractors were called in to restore water and fence. Rudy contacted his pal Jack to say that it seemed the bull liked his former girlfriends better than the young heifers, and would he please keep his animal and his suggestions on his side of the fence!

The neighborhood returned to peace and harmony, with the newly minted rancher neighbors remaining friends, but without exchanging cattle advice. Jack did hire some real cowboys who gathered up the bull and trucked it off to the Buellton sales yard. He had come to realize that bulls and casual part-time ranching life don't mix all that well.

Those of us who have moved into the Valley to take up ranching and made all the dumb mistakes of learners know that the real ranchers and cowboys tell tales and laugh at us gringos coming in from the city streets. However, in our friendly Valley, there are no grudges or mean spirits, and we all get along together.

Close Encounters

Valley animals and Valley people cross paths, often in surprising and memorable fashion. Here are a couple of the incidents that are not enough for an episode, but still part of the warp and woof of our community life.

John and Georgia Wiester were driving home late from an evening out when they were astonished to see a large black form leap from the side of the road, over their cattle guard, and into their farmyard. On arriving home, John brought out their two house dogs, a Jack Russell and a Shepherd, on leashes to investigate what he thought might be a bear. No bears had been seen in his ranch area along Santa Rosa Road, but this was a possibility. True to form, the Jack Russell bristled and communicated, "Let me at 'em!" and the Shepherd hung back and communicated, "Nothing to be concerned about here!" John wisely followed the loyal Shepherd's advice and left the bear form to its own devices, but remained curious.

In the following days, he asked neighbor ranchers if they had spotted anything that might resemble a large bear and discovered that, yes, there had been glimpses and dog alerts, and the neighborhood sensed that an intruder was indeed tramping the trails. Finally, some time later, a neighboring ranch had experienced a Loomix trough mostly destroyed by a mysterious force. Loomix is a cattle-feeding supplement put out for growth and health in large plastic containers about two feet by six, and a foot and a half deep. The consistency of the mix is a molasses-like sticky goo full of nutrients. If indeed a bear came upon the trough, it would seem to be the ultimate honey pot, and very tempting.

The saga seemed to end when another neighbor spotted what was surely a large animal, coated in mud by what must have been sticky Loomix well layered in caked-on dirt, and perhaps the most dirty and disheveled bear in the world. That was the last sign of a bear on Santa Rosa Road. Bears can swim, and we can only hope that this greedy intruder found his way to a Santa Ynez River pool for a long, cleansing swim before a hike to bear territory in the Los Padres National Forest.

Another friend and neighbor of John Wiester was a city type who had bought some property in ranchland by way of escape from the bustle. One night, the new owner turned in to his property and somehow hit and injured a young (fortunately) mountain lion. The man (who shall remain nameless) loaded the limp and barely conscious lion cub into his car and raced to the nearest vet, who reluctantly took on the case and began treatment for a broken leg and other injuries that proved curable. The new property owner had the satisfaction of rescuing his injured young lion, and had also incurred significant vet bills for his trouble.

Some months later, after the medical costs were paid, the now healthy, growing animal living in a cage in the garage was very much on the man's mind. He tried unsuccessfully to place the lion in a zoo, and found very little other interest for adoption. The young and growing lion obviously did not want to play or be petted, and, in fact, the city dweller began to have some fears for their future relationship. Finally, in desperation, our well-intentioned rescuer turned to the California Department of Fish and Wildlife, and two agents soon arrived and surveyed the lion situation.

They agreed that, indeed, the animal had no future in the garage or in domestic life, and took custody to remove the growing beast. What they knew and what the newcomer to the Valley did not know is that any wild mountain lion who has had extensive contact with people cannot be let loose in the wild, and is a condemned being. The wardens summarily shot the lion before driving off to dispose of the carcass, leaving our well-intentioned newcomer sad, out the vet bills, and wiser to the ways of the country.

Fantasy Mare

Most trainers and cowboys who have worked with horses all their lives will tell you that they know much about horses, but they do not really know what horses think. Horses will accept training and willingly do what they have been taught, but what they think about is a mystery. There is one horse, however, whose thoughts are readily recognizable. A Belgian Zangersheide stallion named Jaguar who lives in Hope Ranch and travels occasionally to the Valley for stallion breeding business thinks about female horses, and has fallen in love in a unique horsey way.

The Bidwells live in Santa Barbara with two daughters who are first-class riders as is their mother, Geri Bidwell. This family has taken on one of the most dangerous and demanding horse show events, open jumping, and won impressive victories in shows around the country.

The high jump event is the most exciting crowd-pleaser in horse shows because it involves spectacular jumping over decorated and formidably dangerous obstacles. Another event, the hunter class, involves low jumps, and the emphasis is on style and way of going. But the open jumping event is a free-for-all, with competitors soaring over impossible-looking barriers any way and at any speed. A clean jump is a joy, and knocking a pole down is easily recognizable by the crowd, holding its collective breath and watching horse and rider negotiate the difficult jump course. The horses are big and beautiful and well turned out. The riders exhibit skill and courage, and are sometimes seemingly frail, beautiful, and well-turned-out women. This event is often the high point of a horse show, with spectators alternately suspended in a tense silence, bursting into cheers with a clean go, and groaning when a bar is knocked down or a horse refuses to jump the obstacle. Occasionally, there is also a crash with the rider carried out on a stretcher.

Geri's husband well remembers sitting in the grandstand, holding their then young two daughters, and watching his wife in her early days of competition. She was scheduled third in order for the high-jump class. The first horse crashed the obstacle right in front of where they were sitting and never attempted another try. The second horse crashed the

obstacle, and the rider was carried off in an ambulance. Next to go, Geri made the course without mishap, but her more sober-minded husband can be forgiven for wondering what this was all about.

Obviously, the horse is crucial to jumping success, and the Bidwells search the world for talent.

In the dark ages, armored knights battled each other for honor and territory. The charge of heavily clad mounted warriors often decided kingdoms and dynasties. The all-important vehicle for a knight was the strong and willing warhorse who could carry armored weight into battle and not shy from opposing mounted knights and spears. It takes a certain mindset to be a warhorse, and large, strong-bodied, and iron-willed horses were bred in Europe and sold for, as they say, "a knight's ransom."

These willing and athletic horses have been bred through generations, and now are found competing in show rings and Olympic Games jumping events. Some of the best come from a corner of Belgium, famous for their courage and agility. The Belgian Zangersheide breed certainly boasts a warhorse heritage, because these horses willingly charge and leap with courage and gusto.

The Bidwells' daughters had grown up to show also, and enjoyed success, winning with two Zangersheide mares in classes around the country. The family decided to bring the stallion sire of the mares from Belgium to perpetuate the successful jumping breed. They traveled to Belgium and sought out the relation to their two mares, a magnificent 17.2-hand gray stallion named Jaguar Van Paemel. The sale was agreed on, and the horse flew to California, suffered the required quarantine, and moved to the Hope Ranch stable. Soon the fun began.

Stallions are never easy, and horse sense, concentration, and courage are required to handle the spirited animals. One must never turn a back or lose focus while leading a stallion into or out of a stall. Once Geri turned to answer a question, and the huge Jaguar shouldered her down and walked right over her, fortunately only leaving a couple of bruises. But the stallion was not mean, only energetic, and could be ridden at home and driven periodically to the Valley to deliver the breeding potion that was carefully extracted and handled by the Herthels' Alamo Pintado Equine Medical Center. There was a good market for this breeding potential around the country, and all seemed peaceful in the stable. But a problem developed.

The Bidwells had inherited a beautiful large painting of a lovely mare in a farm field. The realistic painting of the white female horse on a green background measured six by six feet and was too large for any wall in their home. After some thought, they settled on the stable, which was neat and presentable, with large wall space. The painting was perfect and happily decorated a large empty panel. However, by pure chance, the painting hung on a wall opposite the spacious stall that Jaguar the stallion came to call home in California. Who would have thought that a horse would eyeball the painting and ultimately fall in love with the image of the stunning white mare?

Perhaps the Bidwells and crew should have paid closer attention to the romantic horsey nickers and snorts, and also some show-off prancing emanating from the stall, as the painting played with Jaguar's mind. The large stallion was thinking honeymoon, and stallion love is a forceful presence.

One day Geri came to lead Jaguar out to a paddock, and the stallion lost all composure. The huge animal began dancing on his hind legs, rear hooves making a clop, clop sound on the brick stable floor. His flailing front legs dashed in the air as he moved to mount the mare painting. Horse people who handle studs in the breeding shed can imagine the threat, power, and persistence that this eager monster presented. The horse reared and fretted, rising on his back feet and pawing the air. He managed to take a chunk out of the mare's portrait before Geri was lucky and determined enough to handle him back into the stall and lock the lovesick horse out of reach of his paramour. She was fortunate to come out unscathed from this fantasy encounter that was all too real in Jaguar's mind. Geri called for help, and the stud horse only settled when the painting was covered by a horse blanket.

But once again, another day, the blanket blew aside, and Jaguar pranced and nickered, calling to his painted love and threatening to tear the barn down. The blanket was replaced with a large piece of material carefully stapled to cover the unresponsive but attractive female horse. From then on, the painting remained well covered, and our hero, Jaguar, could only dream of the beautiful but silent lady across the way.

Peace has settled on the Bidwell spread, with Geri occasionally riding the beautiful animal, and Jaguar looking forward to his trips to the Valley to donate his stallion seed to mares around the country who will hopefully produce generations of talented jumping horses. If there is a lesson here, it is perhaps that breeding stud farms across the country who might need inspiration for shy stallions would do well with paintings of attractive mares in the barns.

Happy Trails

The ways of the Old West are mostly lost to city folks, except in Western films, but a longing for the cowboy life still lurks in the minds and vacation dreams of urban dwellers. A famous and satisfying establishment to realize those dreams for families, celebrities, and cowboy wannabes alike is the Valley's Alisal Guest Ranch & Resort. This family-owned ranch initiated hotel accommodation in 1946, and still offers fresh air, great dining, tennis, golf, fishing, spa treatment, a host of entertainments, and—best of all, in keeping with the unique ranch property and ranching tradition—horseback trail rides.

The availability for these rides requires a large string of willing horses and personable and experienced wranglers to run the operation. A critical responsibility of the staff is to search far and wide for suitable mounts for a safe and enjoyable dude ranch experience. No small talent is exacted by the wranglers in providing horses and outings for a range of guests, aged seven years to ninety, some without the slightest riding knowledge or experience and others who claim to be champion riders.

A typical ranch guest will sign up for a trail ride in the evening dining room, according to "beginner," "intermediate," or "experienced" skills. Inexperienced guests might exaggerate, while savvy guests often hide their riding background, and it is up to the wranglers to sort out who knows what to ensure the maximum survival. The next day, after a splendid cowboy breakfast, the dudes will saunter along to the corrals to meet their horse assignments. The experienced staff quickly sum up a guest's gear, mannerisms, and mounting approach in order to confirm that horse, ride skill designation, and guest are a safe and compatible match. Then the ride starts off, and the fun begins, with a wrangler in the lead and sometimes another at the back of the single-file, nose-to-tail trek.

The guests are in for spectacular scenery, good vibrations of horse therapy, opportunity to see wildlife and cattle, and a shared adventure with family and friends. The wranglers mostly are thinking of guest survival. Beginners will walk and talk, intermediates will trot and perhaps canter, and the advanced group will canter and travel more adventuresome trails.

Once a boastful man irritated the wranglers with his tales of riding expertise and claims that he could ride anything. One wrangler, who was promptly let go afterward, gave him an "anything" but was duly apologetic and distressed when the bandit horse put the rider in his place on the ground. Another wrangler had three young athletic and enthusiastic boys who wanted to gallop. They set off at a fast canter, but in this rare instance the horse ran away with the wrangler, who dashed ahead and out of sight until he could find a hill and a fence to stop the escape. He looked back in fear for his young guests, but they soon appeared whooping and hollering that this was the best ride they had ever had. The wrangler relaxed, and his runaway horse was sold down the line to a hardened cowboy on another working cattle ranch.

Sometimes guest riders insist on going their own way. On one occasion in the experienced group, a rider, even after being warned, slipped away from the others and tried to water her horse in Alisal Lake. The soft mud at the edge sucked the front hoofs in, and the horse reared back, landing the startled rider in the muck. All the wranglers carry radios, and a call for help brought a truck to carry the sodden and splattered dude back home to her shower. Another trail-wise wrangler once counseled a guest who had won many ribbons in the horse show ring: "Just tell 'em you rode some when you were young, so they'll give you a calm horse, and enjoy the scenery!" That sounds like advice for a great ride.

Many guests tend to return to the Alisal again and again, sometimes with new family generations. I met one man who had ridden the Alisal's trails for years, but gave me an early-days horror story of his beginner ride, very atypical of the ranch. A new wrangler took out some inexperienced riders and thought that the routine included a canter. When he sped up the group of novices, three fell off, fortunately on soft earth, and he had to call for backup to corral the horses and help the fallen. The rescue driver switched places with the wrangler, who drove a shaken-up guest back to the stables. By the time the group rode back to the ranch, the original new wrangler was seen driving out in his car with his bags packed. He had been fired on the spot for his untimely speed-up.

A much more typical ride involved me, the granddad, and two of my grandchildren, aged ten and twelve. They had only a passing experience with riding, but the knowledgeable wranglers put them on totally sympathetic horses and charming guides led us on a scenic walk around the ranch to my delight and to the thrill of my two. The only problem occurred when old granddad, despite riding all his life and spending twenty-five years on his own working cattle ranch, but with ten years not riding, experienced some tired and sore leg muscles.

The Alisal is not only a guest ranch getaway but also a working cattle ranch with over ten thousand acres of commercial operation. One of the special riding features is the opportunity for guests to gather a small herd of cattle from an upper pasture and drive them into a ranch corral, where they are sorted, weighed, and taken out again by the cowboys and dudes. This is as close to the real thing that city dwellers can get without moving to North Dakota and signing on to live in a cold-water bunkhouse.

Coyotes, mountain lions, bears, wild boars, eagles, hawks, and rattlesnakes, as well as the cattle, share the ranch. All of these Wild West animals are seen often, and visitors never know quite what to expect. On one famous trail ride, the guests observed a mountain lion attack and kill a deer. Another quiet ride was threatened by a teeth-barred and growling coyote, with the wrangler concerned it might be rabid until the cubs she was protecting were spotted in the background. The worst trail ride enemies are the ground-living yellow jackets that can be stirred up by the lead horses and then attack the riders behind. The only solution to a swarm of angry stingers is to trot on as fast as possible, hope the guests stay on board, and then search the manes and tails for hangers-on that might sting later and cause a stampede.

In the evening, by the fireplaces of the comfortable bar and dining room, riding tales are exchanged, and aching muscles eased with local wine. The success of the horseback outings are evidenced by the guests riding out the next day. The loyal and workaday horses in the Alisal pasture are true serving Valley animals, adding to the lore and saga of our country.

Part Four

DOMESTIC PARTNERS

Dog Park

Dogs appreciate exercise, and a walk on the road attached to a righteously active owner is a pleasure. But this comes with pavement, traffic, impatient waiting while the boss talks to neighbors, and the ever-present leash. Much greater fun is to be had romping freely on a grassy hill, often in the company of new and old dog friends.

These joyous occasions are found at PAWS Park in Buellton. The dog-friendly space is located on a residential street cul-de-sac, conveniently situated on a sidehill with oak tree shade. In the dedicated, fenced-in area, dogs can be turned out to gamble on the grass with toys, water trough, dog company, and people just standing by watching. Dog happiness is here!

In 2009, local housing developer Fred L. Fredericks received permission to build a number of houses in the city of Buellton. California development is never easy, and part of his settlement with the Buellton city authorities was the donation of excess land on a picturesque hillside that had a brilliant future. The land was found to be too steep for a people park, and the city council came up with a creative and thoughtful Valley solution. A three-acre parcel was deeded, along with considerable grading and preparation, to the city, which then decided, after considerable lobbying from the locals, to dedicate the land not to people, but to dogs.

The Buellton dog park is a joy for pets and people alike. Two well-fenced spaces, one for large dogs (twenty-five pounds and up) and one for small (under twenty-five pounds), are irrigated and planted with grass, supplied with dog toys and tugs, maintained with clean water bowls, securely double gated, and open for all canine comers. It is a thrill to see happy dogs meet each other, sniff, exchange dog sizing up, and then run and play as they will.

Dog owners will bring their leashed animals to the entrance pen and unleash them onto the spacious green hillside where they can romp at pleasure. Some dogs might be intimidated at first by larger and more boisterous new friends, but the visitors soon sort themselves out and run and play with abandon. There are rules and protocols. Loud barking is discouraged. Dogs must not be aggressive and, above all, not be given to fighting. Owners must clean up dog poop. Dogs must be vaccinated and otherwise healthy.

Dog personalities are immediately apparent. Some welcome company, some are shy, some want to win, and some just want to play. Most of the dogs have come to know each other from previous visits, and newcomers are quickly merged. Our Miniature Australian Shepherd, Chelsea, qualified for the over-twenty-five-pounds arena, but was very much on the smaller side for her grouping, and quite intimidated on introduction to the larger players. After about ten minutes of sniffing and backing off, she was soon running with the pack, and even stole a tennis ball from a black Lab.

The park is under the ownership and jurisdiction of the city of Buellton and managed by the parks and recreation department, but the day-to-day upkeep and management is supported by a foundation, appropriately named PAWS, that maintains and operates the facility. The seven board members are Valley animal saints who raise maintenance funds, supervise the park operations, and set the atmosphere for this dog heaven. Linda Hart has been a board member since inception and a regular visitor and supervisor of park operations.

In all her years, Linda has seen only a handful of dogfights or other problems. Aggressive dogs are asked to leave, and if there are any uncooperative owners, the Buellton police are quick to respond and enforce the park behavior rules. Once, a pair of new canine visitors pounced on an unsuspecting dog and cut the victim up enough to require hospitalization. The aggressive pair's owner gave a false phone number and was never seen again, so the PAWS foundation and visitor contributions were required to help with the vet bills. That incident stands out, as there has never been anything like it before or after. Fighting rarely takes place, and if there is a threat, it is soon sorted out, and the participants are excluded.

Just like people, the regular dog visitors tend to select friends and playmates. Some dogs just seem to enjoy the company of other dogs and ignore those they choose not to like. There must also be some pecking order selection, but that is not evident and is a subtle ingredient of the happy dog play. Owners also become friends and enjoy the society of sitting around on the benches while waiting for their pet friends to expel their energy. Sociably watching a free-run dog is much preferable in making friends to just passing by with leashed dogs on the street.

All in all, Buellton's PAWS Park is a splendid addition to the community. The very idea of the park, and the years of volunteer support by the community and PAWS foundation, is a reflection of the relationship of Valley types with their animals. Anyone with a dog friend would do well to make a visit and also pass a contribution to the foundation.

Different Friends

Valley households contain many different assortments of animal members that fulfill unique roles in the people–critter makeup. There is a common Valley culture that desires furry friends to complete a happy home, and these companions come in various shapes and sizes. Two families, with very distinctive animal friends, are something of a departure from normal patterns in Valley life. These unique family members might seem somewhat unusual to outsiders and bizarre to anyone living on Fifth Avenue in New York City.

Mick and Renée Kelleher live on a large plot in a beautiful hillside home off Alamo Pintado Road. Mick, otherwise known in Major League Baseball as "Killer," enjoyed a long career as an infielder with a number of clubs, from the St. Louis Cardinals and the Chicago Cubs to the Detroit Tigers and the Los Angeles Angels, and finally with a career-capping position as first-base coach for the New York Yankees. He moved around 1995 to the Valley, not intending to become a rancher, but ranching came his way in the form of a gift to his wife of a Limousin heifer calf.

Renée named the beguiling creature Betsy Bloomingdale after her donor's mother, and the small animal soon grew to well over a thousand pounds, sported a beautiful expanse of golden-brown coat, developed a heroic appetite, evidenced a happily docile cow personality, and schmoozed into an infinitely lovable, permanent resident. The cow lived at the Kellehers', in a two-acre sidehill paddock, surrounded by a white board-and-wire enclosure.

Visitors were often startled by the substantial animal peering down a hill, with large ears twitching in curiosity and a spacious face whose eyes asked for nourishment. The Limousin breed normally spends most of the day eating up to forty pounds of food and is always hungry. Indeed, Betsy was known to devour fifty pounds of pumpkin at one feasting, and never to turn down a bucket of scraps. Most of her sustenance was supplied by Mick forking in hay twice daily, but additionally all the Kelleher friends had been invited to bring fruit and vegetable leftovers, and some even stopped by the grocer's produce department on their way to visit. A local gardener joined the fun once a week by throwing in grass cuttings. Betsy understood and exploited these routines.

Cows can see and smell very well, and although she might be found sleeping while standing up, Betsy would instantly alert to possible food sources approaching. Gently awake, she would just gaze and chew her cow cud, but sensing food arrival, she would saunter or gallop down the slalom path to greet a visitor with a sympathetic but hugely demanding face. Betsy showered a cow tendency of heroic slobber in anticipation of a treat, and also might heave a contented bovine sigh and roll of the dark, saucer eyes whilst munching. She never thought of roaming, as everything for her contentment was supplied. Nor had she ever honeymooned with a Limousin bull, so there was no question of milking.

Renée would scratch the nodding head and laugh with Betsy, and pursue her painting avocation in a studio where she could watch her happy cow. Mick would occasionally wave his arms at the animal, sometimes receiving a response in the positioning of Betsy's ears. The hay was served according to Mick's schedule, and Betsy liked it early, sometimes showing frustration if feeding came later in the day or evening. While fielding baseballs in stadiums around the country, Mick probably never dreamed of befriending a large cow. But such is Valley life, and a cow-in-residence made the family complete. Alas, Betsy left this world in 2019, and the

Valley and the Kellehers are diminished by her loss.

Some years earlier, another Valley resident, Ragnhild Reif, was standing in line at a local bank when she observed a woman quietly sobbing, in obvious distress. The kind Ragnhild inquired, and learned that the woman's family was selling out and leaving the area, but there was no future place for their pet zebra whom she dearly loved. A conversation ensued, and soon the sympathetic Ragnhild, with an empty paddock on her ten-acre homestead and no other animals planned for occupancy, agreed to give the zebra a home. Her business-genius husband, Rob, loved his wife and her generous ways with enough patience to welcome the idea, and their two sons thought housing a zebra would be a hoot.

Two days later, a trailer arrived with the zebra plus a surprising, unmentioned goat who kept the zebra company. Ragnhild welcomed the zebra, named Happy, and the goat, named Grumpy, to their new paddock. Rob filled the water tank and threw in some flakes of alfalfa, and the sad and grateful lady drove off to distant parts. The two newcomers did not communicate very much to the outside world, but settled in nonetheless.

Zebras are startlingly beautiful animals with their horsey features and impressive stripes. They act somewhat like horses except they don't bond with people, will not carry or pull, and will bite or kick suddenly without explanation. They eat hay like a horse, but require no health or hoof care, and independently just get on in their own way. Zebras are not far removed from the African plains, where the animal instinct of suspicion and survival is foremost in the narrow equine mind. Fortunately for goat and zebra, the Reifs were OK with these low returns from the otherwise-picture-perfect zebra–goat family paddock.

All Ragnhild and Rob's efforts at communication or friendship were rebuffed, and the striped animal just got on with being a zebra and looking good as a conversation piece. With coaxing, treats, and some good luck, the Reifs and their two boys were able to pose for an annual Christmas card with Happy and Grumpy, but that was all besides flakes of hay and a little paddock cleanup. Strangers arriving at the Reif home were startled by the unlikely pair, but the two Valley animals just stared back and stayed quiet.

A herd of zebras on the Serengeti plain will graze in a rough circle formation with each animal warily looking out in a different direction.

Lions, jaguars, hyenas, and all else hungrily crave a zebra dinner, and that threat goes on twenty-four hours a day. This circumstance tends to shape an attitude, and no zebra in the Santa Ynez Valley, even totally spoiled by care and feeding, can get over that mindset. A very different Betsy held no ancestral worries of sustenance or threat from lions, so there were no cow concerns in the world to bother her mind. Zebras and Limousins are just different.

Some Valley dwellers enjoy the benign bovine friendship of a companionable cow, and some the wild beauty and narrow mind of an exotic zebra. The Valley continues to contain, as they say, different strokes for different folks.

Family Members

Like many Valley families, the Cassidys have an extensive biography in the outside world, with Shaun's background of acting, singing, scriptwriting, producing, and a famous family heritage. After a career as a teenage idol and actor, Shaun is now more settled as a producer and director, and lives a happy life with four children. The members of this popular family are healthy, normal, and personable—and complete with various adopted animals, including two giant turtles. The hard-shelled creature boarders are very much part of the Cassidy clan.

Turtles come into most families as small aquarium swimmers who slowly grow into grass-feeding land dwellers, and although one does not expect them to develop, grow they do. The Cassidy family turtles, named Happy and Lucky, are over a hundred pounds each and have minds of their own. They contentedly subsist on the lush green lawn but seem to have a longing to wander through any gate left open. Abandoned or somehow-displaced turtles come to rescue families through organizations that seek homes for injured, unwanted, or otherwise-surplus creatures who need a home. The Santa Barbara Wildlife Care Network, in general, and the Santa Barbara organization Turtle Dreams, a tortoise rescue and rehabilitation operation, are two sources for turtle placement into families such as the Cassidys.

Turtles are thought to be about the size of a kitchen pot, but in fact they grow into a formidable 120-pound hard-shelled size. They are believed to be slow moving, but can scamper for short distances at the pace of an old, fat dog. They seem to adapt easily, and the Cassidy pair happily chomp the lawn and bask in the sun, doing their leisurely tortoise thing. Turtles seem to be continually thinking in long, quiet days, but it is not given to us to know the nature of these musings.

Locals are aware of the Cassidy turtles, and one day, Shaun was called out with the alarming news that one of them had escaped, had wandered, and needed to be rescued from the Santa Ynez Feed & Milling Co. parking lot. Amazingly, the large beast seemed to have traveled a few miles from the Cassidy home and across busy streets. Shaun arrived and secured assistance to lift the heavy animal into his truck. Back home, he and his wife, Tracey, wrestled the animal, with the help of some boards as a slide, back into the garden. The turtle seemed to have enjoyed the trip and was unconcerned.

While Shaun was driving, Tracey checked the yard, found no gates open, and, indeed, discovered their two turtles innocently grazing! She also seemed to know her turtle better than her husband. "Honey, that's not our turtle!" she exclaimed after unloading.

"Well," he replied, "it looks like, and now it seems to be, ours." Three giant tortoises now happily grazed the lawn and communed in their turtle way.

Days later, ads in the local paper and posted notices finally brought a phone call. A lady admitted, in a somewhat hesitant manner, that it must be her family's turtle. After some conversation, she finally asked if perhaps the Cassidys would like to keep their new friend. Tracey regretted that two turtles were enough, and the lady finally agreed to come over with her husband—who had a very different attachment to the lost and found turtle—to retrieve their animal.

He ran into the Cassidy yard and hugged the turtle while speaking words of affection and endearment usually reserved only for recovery of lost children or stolen puppies. The man's eyes welled in tears as he showered gratitude on Shaun and Tracey. His wife stood back, less enthusiastic about the reunion, but perhaps realizing for the first time the attachment between her husband and the huge shellback. The tortoise comfortably and unemotionally returned to the husband's care, and the couple drove off with a load of turtle in the back of their truck. The lost and found adventure turned out well, because the new turtle was not really part of the family like Happy and Lucky, but no one really knows what turtles think.

Previous Cassidy family rescue animals have included some goats that contentedly lived and played in the yard. One memorable and popular character named Cody was taken in as a young orphan, bottle-raised, and completely bonded to humans generally and Tracey particularly. Playful and affectionate, he would mooch a carrot or candy bar without apology, and the four Cassidy children were a generous source. He lived years with the growing family and was a fully adopted member of the clan. Finally, he became aged, and his health declined. The vet gave his sad opinion that there was not one thing wrong with Cody, there were many things going wrong, and the blanket diagnosis was simply old age. Cody became less playful, but even more affectionate and emotionally needy.

Eventually the time arrived when Cody was clearly on his last shaky legs. One of the unfair facts of nature is that we people mostly outlive our beloved animal friends. Tracey and the family bedded him in straw, bottle-fed him, and tried every remedy, but the sad ending loomed soon and sure. In the middle of one night, Tracey woke with a sense of dread, dressed warmly, and snuck out to her wheezing goat friend who struggled for air. She curled up beside him on the straw and spoke soothing goat–people words until she heard her friend's last breath. We all may wish for such a sympathetic watcher as Tracey when we pass from this earth.

The Cassidys are known by neighbors, friends, and Valley people as a bright, attractive, accomplished, successful, and friendly family. Also, in keeping with Valley aura, their children have been brought up to know, respect, and love animals that have included pigs, ducks, rabbits, chickens, and the aforementioned turtles and goats. These young might grow into the world of show business or otherwise in the outside world, but they will always be grounded in the Valley tradition of animal partnership. And that is a good thing.

· **F** ·

Virgil Muse

Our Valley hills have a history of people hiding out. Over the years, celebrities and fugitives have nestled in our environs, from stagecoach robbers to amorous Hollywood types hoping to escape detection, often sought by the law or the paparazzi. In the tradition of these hideouts, we currently have a celebrity actor–author who shelters to seek peace and quiet from the bustle of the world to write best-selling novels. But she cannot escape on her own. True to the tradition of animal participation in Valley life, her cat companion and muse is always with her.

Years ago, Fannie Flagg departed her Birmingham, Alabama, roots with her redheaded glamor and incisive wit for the bright lights of New York and Hollywood and a successful career in acting, game shows, and later writing books. Early in her acting career, a producer spotted her writing talents and hired her to do scripts. TV and screenplay writing led her to writing novels, and she hit the big time with her famous Fried Green Tomatoes at the Whistle Stop Cafe, which sold a ton of copies and inspired an Oscar-nominated film. She has many more books in her future, and that is what leads her to the Valley and seclusion. But she does not come alone.

Cats have always been in her life, and a generation ago, an empty nest brought her to a Montecito pet store where a yellow kitten playing with a pencil brought instant love at first sight. For the next nineteen years, the cat, who became known as Henry, was a constant companion, and the two were inseparable. When Henry finally went to the great beyond, Fannie was devastated and lonely, and found that her creative abilities were somehow diminished. Her writing just seemed to dry up without a cat friend to talk with. She struggled on, convinced that there would never be another Henry, until she happened to read a Craigslist ad for a kitten that was in a temporary shelter and very much up for adoption.

Despite her reservations, something compelled her to drive to San Luis Obispo to meet her future. She met a large orange-colored kitten, and somehow the two immediately bonded. They drove back home to Santa Barbara, exchanging mutual noises about a life together. As a bonus, Fannie soon found that her creative abilities returned, and her writing career came alive again.

The orange kitten found himself with the heavy-duty name Virgil, from the ancient Greek poet, which became appropriate as he assumed the position of inspirational muse as well as cat companion. Just as Ernest Hemingway's six-toed cat named Snow White brought him inspiration and fame, why not the same for an adopted orange kitten? Virgil and Fannie soon grew a loving and creative bond, and the kitten settled down to become a cat, but not without a surprise.

Virgil outgrew normal cat size, and his growth seemed unnatural and a little alarming. A concerned Fannie consulted a vet, who immediately explained the circumstance. Virgil was actually a Maine Coon variety, and no ordinary cat. The kitten ultimately grew to almost eighteen pounds.

Maine Coons are characters, with high intelligence, and Virgil was no exception. The large animal developed dark orange stripes, which brought on a tigerlike quality to this friendly companion. Maine Coons have doglike characteristics and are extremely loyal and family oriented. Virgil also developed the breed's expressions—vocalizations that are more like the mumblings of a friendly dog than cat pitches. Members of the breed are known as "gentle giants" as they are large and muscular, but once they have eaten aplenty, are convinced all is right with the world, and are comfortable with the person they love, they curl up and exude good vibrations. In Virgil's case, that includes literary inspirations.

The happiest moments for Fannie and Virgil involve the author deep into story writing and the inspirational cat cured up under the desk, urging the story line on. The two live in a Valley hideout rental, away from all everyday distractions of a normal life in Santa Barbara. They both know their assignments in seclusion to be author productive and cat inspirational. We all look forward to many great books. It is totally Valley appropriate that future novels be partially the product of animal input.

Constant Companions

Of all the celebrities that have graced our Valley, Bo Derek is one whose modest ways, pleasant demeanor, community involvement, and luminous beauty have elevated her to be an all-time favorite. After years of starring in films and television shows, she now lives a quiet country life and is very much supported in this by an ancient burro named Machito. Burros, better known in the United States as donkeys, have been carrying burdens for thousands of years. They are smaller than mules, and the scruffy Machito, whose father was a pony, is very much on the smaller side of burros. Bo and Machito are lucky to have found each other.

Bo's film career, influenced and encouraged by her late husband John Derek, hit the big time with her famous role in 10 and has included numerous pictures that have exploited her stunning blue-eyed, blond, and statuesque persona. One film, Bolero, featured her riding ability when she galloped on her high-potency stallion named Mauro. Any man who saw the film or publicity photos of her dashing on this athletic horse, wearing little if any clothing, held the image in his mind forever.

The horse part of the scene, Mauro, was a stunning white Lusitano stallion. The Portuguese Lusitano breed is as ancient as cave paintings, and has been used through the ages for war, bullfighting, and now numerous horse show and carriage events. These high-spirited horses were never meant for pony clubs, but rather perform for an accomplished rider who wants to show off a picturesque athlete born for photographs. To ride one at a gallop, nearly naked, and without a saddle is the stuff dreams or accidents are made of, and Bo did it in a memorable fashion.

Her secret weapon in preparing for the famous Mauro scene was Valley horseman and trainer Ramon Becerra, a horse whisperer if there ever was one. He has taught horses to perform jumping, dancing, lying down flat, standing still while he does roping tricks standing on the saddle, and a host of other acts. Ramon gave Bo the ability and confidence to ride the high-spirited horse, but he also knew that Mauro needed a little calming to handle the film scene as well as life in general.

The stallion, new to Bo, had become a handful. Mauro's problem was an aggravated nervous disposition that caused him to run up and down the paddock fence, snorting, fretting, and prancing. The horse was losing weight and seemed to be headed for a nervous breakdown, and certainly would be dangerous for Bo to ride. Something needed to be done.

Ramon had helped a number of high-goal polo players from Argentina import energetic horses to North America to play world-class polo. To comfort these athletic horses during their plane or boat shipments from South America, he had often provided laid-back burros as a calming influence. These nonthreatening animals were able to convince horses to travel safely and often proved a good influence in the stables as well. He had noticed one intelligent burro who seemed to be able to fill the settling role with great understanding, and he kept that animal for future assignments. This was the undersized, white-colored, wise-beyond-his-flappy-ears burro named Machito who clearly had demonstrated an ability to get along with horses. He brought Machito to Bo to calm the feisty Mauro, and life began anew.

Ramon and Bo unloaded the burro from a small trailer, and the diminutive animal was led into the paddock to meet the stomping and fretting Mauro. Horse and burro eyed each other, briefly sniffed, and some

vibrations passed between the two. Mauro sighed and calmly strolled around the paddock, casually chomping grass with Machito ambling along behind. The two became inseparable, as though they had known each other forever, and peace and harmony reigned at Bo's ranch. When the time came for the big scene to be filmed, Mauro was an angel.

Understanding the importance of the relationship, Ramon gave the burro to the glamorous actress, and the two lived happily until fifteen years later when Mauro went to horse heaven. Now, in 2020, Machito only has Bo and a couple of polite horses for company. Once, just for fun, Bo tried to ride Machito, and the placid burro gave her one of the worst riding falls she had ever experienced. Being thrown by a burro was as bad as being bitten by a tiger during the production of the film Tarzan. Another time, Bo tried to lead Machito where he did not want to go and wound up being dragged through the mud. The burro was a friend, but very independent.

There is a Western expression for old-time dwellers on a ranch property who have been there so long they have become part of the land: they are called Ranch Indians. These dwellers have a bedrock attachment to the land, and go with the property. The ancient Machito is the soul of a Ranch Indian on Bo's establishment, now and forever.

Ranch owner Bo is a true Valley character, a celebrity, a skilled rider, and very much in tune with animal characters. That is who the Valley is.

Fish Food

Don and Susan Krog have retired to the Alisal Guest Ranch & Resort, Don nearing his nineties and living with the disadvantage of severe eye problems that afflict his vision. They built a charming garden fronting Rancho Alisal Drive, which enjoys heavy people and dog walking traffic, and included a bench for resting along the way.

Sue has a friendly and rambunctious Boxer named Alex that provides her exercise by leading her around the ranch roads and periodically breaking loose to provide friendly chase scenes. Don also longed for animal company, and he finally settled on building a koi pond to house a sociable school of friendly fish.

Don is not given to doing things by halves, and he created a large pond with rock formations and circulating fresh water. Many Valley craftsmen and artisans were delighted with the construction challenges and wages to produce this beautiful front-yard pond, and the result was impressive. After the tanks of pet stores, the Krogs' pond was paradise for the imported fish friends. The design included ledges and underwater hiding areas that everyone thought would provide safe havens for the fish. The birds and raccoons thought differently.

Don purchased some valuable koi and a small herd of goldfish to keep them company. He enjoyed the pond serenity and, especially because of his sight impairment, the multicolored fish creating ripples on the surface and making splashing sounds. His greatest pleasure was sitting on a bench, close to the water, and casting in pellets of food to tempt the fish out, stirring up ripples and splashes as they fed. In the early days, all went happily according to plan. But meanwhile, the neighboring birds and raccoons were salivating and stalking the pond.

Little by little, the fish seemed to diminish, pursued by the predators, and the Krogs wondered if the newcomer swimmers knew to avoid capture in their hiding places. The only explanation was that the plunging birds and the stealthy raccoons were outsmarting the fish, and there was occasional sad evidence of this. The worst moment of this drama occurred when Sue was out walking with Alex. He strained to reach some bushes, and finally snuffled into the foliage. Sue peered in to discover the attraction and sadly saw the remains of a brightly colored and hundred-dollar koi, dropped by some fleeing marauder. The birds and raccoons were winning.

At last Frank Renfro, the Krogs' landscaper, came up with the idea of stringing fishing line across the pond. Accordingly, he pounded stakes around the perimeter and tightly strung the line to create squares of protective wire baffle. Additionally, the Krogs increased the rock shelters and installed censors that would turn on lights to scare off the raccoons.

As of this writing, and last seen, Don was happily sitting on his bench talking to the remaining wary koi and goldfish as they splashed and enjoyed scatters of food pellets. The Darwinian pond struggle will doubtless continue, and we can only hope that the birds and raccoons remove their fishing trips to the Valley lakes.

Chelsea Care

Over the years, the medical community has come to realize the therapeutic benefits of introducing dogs into the healing process. A sympathetic dog can relieve stress and promote a positive outlook that is helpful in recoveries. Most dogs can approach a person suffering from some debilitation, look that patient in the eye, and seem to say, "I don't know you, human, but I would like to be your friend and I hope you get better!" This unconditional love is good medicine.

Among those dogs that evidence this sympathy, there are a number of degrees and certifications. A Seeing Eye® dog is a highly trained specialty dog dedicated to helping a person whose sight is impaired. Then there are many types of "emotional support animals," including service dogs, that are simply special animal friends of a person, sometimes with the certification to gain access to planes, beaches, and hotels from which other pets are barred. The airlines are cracking down on this certification that occasionally becomes a free-riding scam, and are now very particular about the qualifications of canine passengers.

A true Therapy Dog has been trained and certified to work in institutions along with a volunteer handler and is able to function as a valuable member of the caregiver team. To quote from the 2017 Therapy Dogs International (TDI®) handbook: "Therapy Dog visitations can be used to motivate patients, improve socialization, encourage appropriate behavior, develop hobbies, help with relaxation, [and] promote reality orientation, and [a Therapy Dog visit] is a much needed diversion from patients' problems" (p. 9).1

I watched a beneficial Therapy Dog encounter when I was visiting my friend John Cochrane in the Santa Barbara Cottage Hospital rehabilitation unit. John was recovering from a recent vehicle accident that had bruised his body and broken his neck. He was fortunate that there would be no permanent damage, but there would be a slow road to recovery, stuck in a hospital bed. As we were visiting in his hospital room, a smiling handler and a happy Golden Retriever entered, unannounced. The dog seemed to know exactly what to do and padded up to the bed and laid his head on the mattress near John's hand, waiting to be petted. As dog–man greetings and affection were exchanged, the retriever looked into John's eyes and seemed to say, "I hope you are feeling better, old man!" The healing might be long and hard, but the dog had certainly helped the process along as he wagged his tail and padded out to find other patients.

Over our years in the Valley, Kate, the family, and I have had the joy of housing four Shepherd dogs, Daisey, Bumper, MacDog, and Tucker. Each was part of the family and a character in her or his loving, separate way. We outlived them all, and then in our retirement Kate and I concluded that we had been blessed in Shepherd dogs and would hold their memories without more dog friends. Our knowing son Adam thought differently and surprised us one day with a package that sported a Miniature American Shepherd puppy head peering out at us. Of course we were had, and Chelsea came into our lives.

Chelsea was born just outside Buellton on Highway 246 where the Timeless Kennel breeds Miniature American Shepherds, also known as Mini Aussies, and I defy anyone to visit the place and not fall in love with the puppies. They exude friendly, lovable vibrations and are the soul of cute. Our good-looking, tricolor pup was named Chelsea after her mother, and also from the glamorous London township that reflects Kate's English heritage. She adapted quickly to our household ways with hardly any bad habits, plus the minimum of poop and pee, and after a few naughty chews settled in on our laps and in our hearts. By the age of three, she became a conversant family member.

Kate and I had long planned for the possibility of moving to a retirement-type facility in Santa Barbara, a friendly, comfortable place with many living advantages for senior types, but with the one problem of not allowing pets for the residents. We pondered this crisis long and hard, because we were now a family of three and could not imagine life without our Chelsea. However, we learned the one pet exception would be for a Therapy Dog who would visit the residents of the long-term and assisted care unit of our residence facility. We thus undertook the challenge of training and qualifying, hoping that Chelsea was up to the task and would understand the need for this status.

The first stage of the Therapy Dog quest was for Chelsea to become a certified Canine Good Citizen. This status is awarded by the American Kennel Club with a strict examination after months of training. Here, a dog must evidence manners and attention to the handler, and not show tendencies of excitement, wandering, or careless inattention. A good deal of this is in the nature of the dog, and many are just not born and bred to behave. For those who do bond and listen, training involves heeling, sitting, staying in place, and, above all, paying attention to the handler.

We were lucky to find an experienced and sympathetic trainer, Cornelia Martin, who worked hard to educate both Chelsea and ourselves on the ways of good citizenship. Over about five months of off and on training sessions, a very patient and conscientious mom, a largely bystander dad, and a slightly bemused but willing dog learned their stuff, and the day of testing finally arrived.

TDI maintains certified judges who evaluate the potential dog recruits at their various levels of training. Judge Ava Kearnn was all business with Chelsea and one other dog when they were finally ready for citizenship testing. After a close scrutiny of general attitude and manners, the dogs were made to heel, sit, stay, tolerate visitors, and not be upset by strange noises or activities. Both dogs passed after a half-hour of exercises, and Chelsea's Canine Good Citizen diploma hangs framed in our kitchen. She was on her way to Therapy Dog.

The next training was much more of the same, but with higher standards and more emphasis on dealing with unfamiliar people, food lying on the ground that must not be eaten, and garbage can lids (simulating bedpans) being dropped on the driveway. The final exam was strict and longer than the citizenship test, but somewhat eased by being in the company of three dogs that the same judge, Ava Kearnn, now knew by reputation and was inclined to pass. Chelsea took the exam with flying colors, and a second diploma is on the wall, along with a badge and scarf to identify her as a true Therapy Dog.

Chelsea's visitation debut was an invitation to Friendship House, a retirement facility in the Valley. Kate and Chelsea arrived to find a room with twenty or so elderly residents, four in wheelchairs, seated in a circle to greet the new Therapy Dog. They had been alerted that this was the dog's first experience after graduation, and they were looking forward to meeting a new dog friend.

To the facility supervisor's approval and satisfaction, Chelsea immediately wagged her bobbed tail and sidled up to each of the welcoming residents in turn during a half-hour visit. Each resident stroked her rich fur, and Chelsea returned a loving dog look. Kate explained where Chelsea had come from, what her training entailed, and what she hoped to achieve by sitting with and nuzzling the elderly folk. The visit was a total success with a ray of good dog vibrations radiating the room. Chelsea had now graduated and proved herself for a future of Therapy Dog visitations!

Chelsea plans to move into the facility in Santa Barbara with us and pursue her medical career.

NOTE: 1. THERAPY DOGS INTERNATIONAL. (2017). ASSOCIATE MEMBER'S GUIDE (16TH REV. ED.). FLANDERS, NJ: AUTHOR. AVAILABLE FROM HTTP://WWW.TDI-DOG.ORG/ FORMS/MEMBERGUIDE.PDF.

Helen's Homes

Cat thinking is distant and exotic, and, unlike dogs who are up front and obvious, cats just maintain their privacy. One cat resident of Los Olivos, named Helen, personifies feline life.

Helen lived with a happy family in upper Los Olivos. In 2016, she suffered the fate of some unlucky animal residents when her adopted family moved on. When the moment of leaving for a new and distant home arrived, Helen did what cats do and hid. After searching everywhere for their cat and suffering a substantial delay, the family gave up, accepting that Helen just did not want to go.

What must our Valley cat have thought, watching her host family pack up, move the furniture, and then finally drive down the road? Whether this was a deliberate family reduction, or simply the result of an indifferent cat hiding in the bushes from another car trip, we will never understand. The result, either way, was a neighborhood orphan.

We are not to know the cat musings of this silent observer, but can imagine the stoical pondering when dinnertime came and the former home stayed still. If ever the cat trusted people and fate previously, the world was now a lonely and tenuous place. As the days passed, options were weighed behind the searching cat eyes. The odd mouse or bird might serve for a meal, but this could hardly replace regular chow and the chance to come in out of the rain. Independence has a price.

The St. Mark's-in-the-Valley rector, Reverend Randall Day, a sympathetic character and good neighbor, lived across the street and knew all about the family's move, as he had given them hearty goodbyes and blessings. Perhaps this was observed by our stealthy cat, but dismissed

as an extraneous people thing. Also living at the Day house was a much-loved and very spoiled small white Bichon Frisé named Ike, the resident dog. This appealing white bundle of friendship arrived to the good priest through a rescue facility and became a very much-beloved fixture at St. Mark's. As the days went on, the lonely cat observed the dog enjoying food, shelter, warm bed, and constant companionship.

Randall began noticing the cat physically deteriorating with scant food and lonely exposure, but never able to come out of hiding and say hello. When he could stand the sight no longer, he invested in a can of cat food. When the saving bowl was presented before the grassy hideout, the cat vanished. However, later the meal also vanished, and the good deed was tentatively accepted. As the days progressed, the meals were presented and stealthily consumed, and fleeting glimpses of Helen revealed a healthier animal. The hidden cat began to look forward to the nurturing bowl, but also rebuffed any communication with her benefactor, turning her back and retreating from any sign of affection.

Soon the Day side of the street noticed that the cat was watching their front door. Helen could not help seeing that the bowl originated from across the street, and to hasten the delivery, she finally mooched her way to Randall's porch, now twice a day, for the delicious cat food. But still, there could be no communication, and once, when Randall reached out to stroke what he thought was a lonely soul, the cat vanished like streaked lightning. Another time, an extended hand bringing comfort was answered by a lightning strike that actually drew blood from the Good Samaritan. But meanwhile, a bowl of clean water was added to the porch to be enjoyed instead of the odd scrounging around the neighborhood for a drink. The emotional standoff continued.

Inevitably, the seasons changed, and colder weather set in as the months of Helen indifference became less aggressive while Randall's feeding continued. Now, even the standoffish cat noticed that there was warmth to be had behind the door of the feeding porch and a home enjoyed now only by a dog. Finally, Helen bowed to the inevitable and accepted the invitation to sleep inside, away from wind and weather. At first the overnights were met with stony indifference by Ike the Bichon, but gradually he too warmed to the stray cat known as Helen.

Now, four years later, the cat lives happily in Father Randall's home. The dog offers complete acceptance, offering to play and seeming to say, "Welcome to the family! These people treat you right, and here there's warmth, good food, and love. Come play with me!" Unfortunately, Helen the cat's answer is, inevitably, "Don't mess with me, son! We can be partners, but not friends!" Ike has a hard time understanding. A dog will give affection in abundance, but a cat only seems to accept what suits her mood, and not necessarily what is offered.

But meanwhile there is some hope. Good rector Randall Day will say his daily prayers quietly in his home. Helen has figured out this routine and will usually curl up and doze beside him while this people thing is going on.

· 🅕 ·

Stray Friends

People who live in the Valley are perhaps as ready to help a straying pet as anyone anywhere in the world. Dogs wandering the road or cats showing up at strangers' doors are likely to be welcomed, identified, and returned; many are recognized and brought to their neighborhood homes, some are sheltered until a notice appears, and, as a last resort, a few wind up with Santa Barbara County Animal Services. The lost and found stories are too numerous to recount, but one happily ending tale is both typical and a good lesson in household animal care.

A lovable family member of the Golden Retriever variety had been a ranch dog for many years, helping bring up the children and showering the large spread with good dog vibrations. Named Brophy, he was so much a part of the establishment that the family had become a little careless in details of licensing, identification, immunization, and the likes. He was a beloved part of the ranch and slept in the stable dreaming of the next barbecue. Looking back, the people suspect that a day of rifle target practice may have been the source of his odd behavior, but the net result is that Brophy disappeared.

The dog was old enough to know better, but unlucky enough to wander off the spread, a very unusual pattern. At first there was no concern, with the ranch family thinking that he was just wandering and would turn up the next day, but after he missed two dinners, they began to spread the alarm. Neighbors were called, as were all the likely places that might know something of the good dog's whereabouts. The usual notices were posted, and friends were on the lookout, but after those two nights' absence everyone was worried and began to lose hope. There were predators in the hills and fast cars on the road.

The college-type member of the family was computer savvy and initiated all possible electronic searches. Finally the cloud paid off, and a Facebook posting and good fortune led the search to the Santa Maria Animal Shelter, which replied, "Yes, we have a friendly Golden Retriever–type stray that answers to that description." County Animal Services is a sympathetic and experienced operation, but also no-nonsense, and too often strays have a limited future. Fortunately, the Santa Maria rescuers figured that such an appealing creature must have a home somewhere.

The dog-owning couple dashed up to the shelter, and the dog jumped into their loving arms. Apparently, he had wandered to Highway 154, and an unidentified motorist had picked up the hitchhiker. Brophy, with his trusting nature, had no problem hopping into a strange car, but he had no idea it would be a ride to the county jail. He was safe, but the happy homecoming did not quite end the tale.

The businesslike county shelter had supplied all the necessary immunization, bath, grooming, and board for three days. They also noted that the dog had no county tag, chip, or record of immunization, all of which were supplied by the shelter at retail price, not to mention the license and paperwork that needed to be covered, too. The bill came to something over four hundred dollars for the return of a loving family friend—now legal, clean, and healthy. Tab settled, the united and happy, but wiser, family drove home, complete with wooly friend curled up in the back seat.

Day Walker

Those of us who frequent Los Olivos have long noticed a picturesque, elderly lady leading a troika of picturesque, elderly dogs on the less and less quiet streets, a scene that is pure Norman Rockwell. The lady is Joni Jackson, who has lived in the Valley forever, and the dogs, half Italian Greyhound and half Whippet, are littermates, over sixteen years old, and named Twitter, Beatrice, and Blossom. Joni confesses that the perambulations have been slowing down in recent years.

The elegant mini parade takes a daily route through the Los Olivos roads and pathways, starting out down Alamo Pintado Avenue (the lesser town road, not the greater cross-Valley bikeway that has space for cars and is named Alamo Pintado Road). Joni and her three best friends live with Rebecca Keyko who also houses and walks with her two similar dogs,

Oliver and Lila. But Rebecca has a day job, and not the retired leisure to walk as often as Joni, and her pace is not as measured.

There is something reassuring and Valley satisfying about the quiet presence of Joni Jackson and her dog friends. Many people walk their dogs here, but not usually with three tethered to the same leash and totally content to make their leisurely way on the streets, oblivious of cars. Local drivers know to make a path, and visitors just seem to understand about driving around this senior scene.

Joni readily admits she is getting on, and regrets losing both her husband and Kismet, the father of her three dog companions. Kismet regularly slept with his head on Joni's chest, and sometimes she wonders who she misses the most, her husband or her beloved Kismet, who was perhaps the less restless sleeper.

Though there is no great drama about this dog and matron stroll, the scene has a place in Valley stories because of the very comforting and local nature of the event. May the Valley always celebrate and be road-alert for such a benign happening.

By the way, on passing give the foursome a smile and be sure to slow down.

Turf Wars

If ever there is a householder without a pest problem in the Valley, it will be a miracle. Rats, mice, squirrels, gophers, termites, bats, skunks, ants, and all manner of creepy-crawlies crave to share our space and sustenance. The competition goes on, and we all fight the eternal battle in our own way, but fortunately there are some pros on our side.

Sometimes even strangers invade our lives. As I write, a pesky brown bird has discovered a rival peering out from the reflection in my office window. One doesn't think of birds as pests, but this one periodically pecks away at his reflection, inches from my ears. When I rush out and yell, the bird just poops on my ledge only to resume his pecking once I am settled inside. Maybe the remedy is to paint an ugly face on cardboard taped to the window where the bird reflection occurs. It just might work.

Each season brings a new wave of invasion and reopens the continuing turf battle. For instance, with winter comes the cold weather and shivers to the rodent population. Instinct and common sense draws these heat seekers searching for openings in our homes through an enticing trail of escaping warmth. Mice can sense and enter through a warm whiff only a pencil in diameter, and rats can enter through an opening roughly the size of a twenty-five-cent coin. Once inside, the nooks and crannies of wood construction offer easy living, and there are usually spills and crumbs for nourishment.

Unfortunately, the rodent population both lives and dies in our inner walls, and in dying, the lingering smell can last months. One homeowner tells the story of being driven to distraction by a flesh-decaying odor within, with wife and family threatening to move out to the grandparents' home. After a futile search, he finally summoned a council of war with a home builder and pest management service, and ordered the walls to be ripped apart, even to a major part of the house, to discover the source of the ugly smell. Fortunately, only a closet and bathroom wall needed to be replaced before the burial site was uncovered.

Rick Gillespie is the president of Nu-Tech Pest Management, a combat hero in these homeowner wars, and a good guy to have on our side. Rick is a strong ally in convincing little nasties to go to the beyond or go bother the neighbors. He and his service people regularly patrol residents' properties in the Valley to control and monitor various pest invasions, knowing that they will never win the war, but they can hold the pesky animals outside the house. A background of many years dealing out repellant chemicals, poisons, shock treatment, and closing avenues of entry has earned him the reputation and gratitude of numerous families, now comfortable at home. He is the general, his weapons are many and evolving, and his troops travel the yards and rafters in white suits to fight the wars.

Government agencies serve as something of a referee in these wars, with a constant monitoring and control inspired by environmental and animal protection activists. Bats, for instance, are a protected species. These night flyers can leave a mess of bat poop and regurgitated bug parts, and be a menace to a porch or open overhang roof. The antidote from this endangered species is lighting and nets, which if effectively utilized can persuade the ugly little creatures to chew and evacuate on someone else's property. Wineries have a particular attraction for bats, and here only elaborate netting will send the night flyers back to highway bridges or some other winery.

In past years, a common gopher getter was a shock explosion device that could be set off in tunnels to convince the critters to go elsewhere, if they survived the blast. Rick remembers the sheriff arriving one day to settle the gun battle that had been reported by neighbors when the pest service blasted too loud and too often. This remedy is outlawed today. Rick also remembers past years when pest control people would spray too much chemical, too close to homes, pets, and people, endangering invaders and homeowners alike. Chemical bans, limitations, and restrictions have mostly been a healthy change, even if the scales have tipped in the pests' favor.

Larger infiltrators such as skunks, raccoons, and opossums are mostly trapped and released. All these animals can have an attractive look, and are sometimes fed and encouraged by a homeowner. Rick recalls a family feeding raccoons, who happily accepted potato chips and leftovers until the behavior became a habit. When the family went on vacation, the raccoons just figured the goodies were in the house, available without people service. The clever and muscular raccoon family let themselves in by ripping off a section of the roof, and made themselves at home until the alarmed residents returned and called in the troops with bait and traps. The Nu-Tech trucks relocated the raccoons to the back of Los Padres National Forest, and the family never offered potato chips again!

In a very rare case, the pest management people tell of a skunk that was trapped in an awkward situation only drastic measures could resolve. The service manager (not Rick's firm) called in the most junior control person; gave the young man a protective suit, respirator, and pistol; and sent him in to do the job. He was told that if he got close enough, he could point the pistol at the skunk, and when the skunk sniffed the barrel, "as they always do," he could blow the skunk's head off for an easy disposal. As it turned out, the path to the caged skunk was long and smelly, and the disposal of skunk remains after the delayed shot longer and smellier. Pest control service reps love to tell the story of how the young man stormed back into the manager's office and plunked the revolver down on his desk without removing his suit or mask. The office aroma was a reminder of the incident for many weeks.

Homeowners should know that their desirable turf is coveted by many critters who want to take and not earn their living from a home's warmth and leftovers. If they haven't thought of enlisting the help of a pest management mercenary who knows the way of these wars, it might be a good idea.

True Blue

All dogs are not alike, and canine breeds absolutely offer differing character and characteristics. Hunting breeds want to hunt, guarding breeds want to protect, fighting breeds tussle, couch fashion breeds are happy to wear ribbons, and so on. One of the all-time people-oriented and family-friendly breeds, the Miniature American Shepherd, has evolved right here in our Valley.

The breed development saga began in 1972 when Curtis Taylor, about to be retired from the U.S. Air Force at Vandenberg, noticed and rescued a lost and bleeding puppy from the side of the road. The two bonded, and the pup grew up to be a somewhat undersized but otherwise totally talented and sympathetic dog friend with impressive characteristics. After his discharge, Curtis married Cindy Perron, and the two continued to live in the area with their side-of-the-road stray, now known as Chupanako, Greek for "little shepherd."

By pure chance, and without ambitions, they entered the grown-up pup in a local Lompoc dog show and, even though Chupanako was somewhat undersized, were amazed to find the rescue pup won a best of breed championship. They obtained an Australian Shepherd Club of America registration and bred their dog to a pedigreed and likely lady Shepherd who produced beautiful pups.

One of the pups was given to Cindy's mother, Jeanine Perron, who knew about showing, and Chupanako's descendants also began to win trophies. This pup grew to sire a host of superior offspring who began to establish a dynasty. The breeding program continued, and the family began to realize that they had some beautiful, if traditionally undersized, dogs with somewhat differing behavior and characteristics from the regular Australian Shepherds. The dogs that did not go into the show ring were placed with families and were totally successful in their homes.

The world of breeding purebred dogs is full of regulations, complications, and formalities overseen by the American Kennel Club. When a new variation of animal emerges, with different characteristics from recognized and registered breeds, an enthusiastic following of kennels may well become convinced that they are producing something unique and deserving. The next step, to formal breed recognition, is long and complicated. For instance, the traditional Australian Shepherd breeders were not enthusiastic about a trend to produce something similar but smaller and officially identified differently. A new designation might diminish the Shepherd classification.

However, with persistence, and after a history of advocacy and development, the breeders of these smaller Shepherd dogs finally settled on the designation, Miniature American Shepherd, with all the qualifications and specifications of a new breed. Finally, the advocates successfully obtained full recognition in 2011.

At the forefront of this process were Cindy Perron and her daughter, Karen Keller-Ross, who live in Buellton. Karen is the current president of the Miniature American Shepherd Club of the USA. The work of this local family in establishing a new American breed was historic in the dog world, and allows the Valley to take much credit for the success of establishment and then recognition of these splendid animal companions. As of 2020, there are some thirty-plus Miniature American Shepherds living happily in Valley homes, and more are on their way.

An outstanding representative of this new variety came from a litter of puppies, carefully bred by Karen Keller-Ross, into a young Valley woman's life in 2017. The eight-week-old puppy, named Tallulah Blue, was purchased as a gift by Georgina Walker's parents and is now her complete

soul companion. The pup's status is officially co-ownership, which means that Karen had recognized young Blue as a stellar example of the breed and retained the right to select a sire husband for Blue and own all the progeny of one litter. In due course, she honeymooned and produced six pups in 2020 who have now gone on to be sold into families for two-thousand-dollars-plus or retained for show ring competition.

But now that her contractual obligations are satisfied, this brown-eyed, gray and white bundle of bright, loving energy has completely attached herself to Georgina and fulfills all one could desire in a dog companion. They live together in Los Angeles now. Blue runs the apartment by day, after a brisk morning walk in the suburbs, and looks forward to a run on the beach at night. Sometimes she will bicycle ride in a backpack, and sometimes she will shop, riding in a cart. Best of all, she often returns to visit the Walker family home in the Valley.

Blue knows which people are welcome and who are strangers to be announced with a suspicious bark. She is very conscientious about her personal habits and hygiene, and happily sleeps on the bed with her person. Whenever and whatever life presents, she is ready and willing, and above all wants to do the right thing. She has gone sailing and gone camping; will speak when asked; seems to understand many words; and will lie down, play dead, shake hands, and roll over all in her spare time while wanting to do and understand more. Blue is the perfect companion. Someday, if the family of two ever becomes larger, she will be a complete member.

The Valley can take pride and give thanks that Karen Keller-Ross and her family have developed this splendid breed. And if anyone comes to be the special partner of one of the Miniature American Shepherd tribe, they will owe a vote of gratitude to this local family for developing the heritage of their dog friend.

Petunia's Rescue

Petunia the stray dog was in trouble and abandoned in Bakersfield and fell into the hands of the local Fresno County Humane Animal Services where wayward dogs and cats are too numerous to last long. Fortunately, her good nature and adoption potential were spotted shortly before she was to experience the fate of many dogs and cats who end up in county facilities, and the county people were inspired to find the deserving dog a home. Because of a long-standing relationship between our local society and the Fresno facility, Petunia was transferred to the Santa Ynez Valley Humane Society and a bright future.

Our Valley Humane Society is a private, nonprofit organization that is a hero and savior to animals, and a source of pet joy to many adoptive households. The organization, founded in 1979 and opened as a facility in 1982, is associated with, but independent from, other humane societies. There is a local and independent board of five, chaired for the last six years by Valley realtor Bob Jennings, whose family lives with an adopted Pit Bull and Border Collie. He and the board work hard to raise the funds to keep the facility alive.

There are nine regular staff for this seven-days-a-week operation, and around fifty volunteers. Local philanthropist and rancher Walter Thomson was a major sponsor in the early days, but otherwise the budget of some five hundred thousand dollars is financed by a successful Solvang thrift shop and the generosity of locals and foundations. Donations to national or other humane societies do not help our local society that stands alone.

The facility on Commerce Drive in Buellton is clean and spacious, housing a changing population of cats and dogs that have been given, found, or transferred for care and, hopefully, adoption. Anyone wanting introduction to the boarders is welcome to explore www.syvhumane.org or arrange for a visit; it is easy here to meet a new, and very rewarding, potential member of the family.

Recently, I visited the facility and had a conversation with Jewel, a big-eyed female cat who yearned to join a loving home and earnestly communicated in her cat way with me about that possibility. Unfortunately, our situation has no chance of including a cat. Beware visiting the Valley Humane Society lest your family be tempted to expand with a delightful and gratifying adoption!

The staff are friendly and helpful, and busily engaged in matchmaking and animal health services including inoculations, cleaning and grooming, spaying and neutering, and other more serious ministrations. No one will receive an unhealthy new pet to take home. These health services are also available for drop-in customers at modest pricing. Visitors regularly stop by to meet the animal residents and possibly adopt, and the staff are happy to help guide families and animals into potential relationships.

One of their notable successes involved a mixed breed who proved too bright and energetic for the average family, but was spotted by a dog enforcement facility in Southern California. After over a year's training, the dog, named Corvin, is a valued member, with a partner/deputy, of the San Luis Obispo County Sheriff's Office force on bomb- and contraband-sniffing duty.

Petunia presented a different situation when she was discovered to be very much in a family way. When good fortune transferred her to the Santa Ynez Valley Humane Society, she soon delivered ten pups! Her offspring prospered and, with Petunia's appealing nature, were sure to find new adoptive homes. Fortunately, puppies are the easiest candidates for adoption.

In Petunia's honor, all of her pups were given flower names to carry to their new families. The Valley Humane Society people had discovered that she was 25 percent Boxer, 25 percent German Shepherd, 12.5 percent Chesapeake Bay Retriever, and 37.5 percent "Herder/Asian." The father of her puppies was thought to be a German Shepherd, but whatever the lineage, the pups soon found happy homes in the Valley. Now it was Petunia's turn—bathed, clipped, spayed, inoculated, healthy, and friendly, she was also adopted after housing had been secured for all her offspring.

Kevin and Yvette Winn live in Solvang and have big hearts, a warm dog-friendly home, and a large space to accommodate dogs in the family. Their own mixed breed named Brewster, previously adopted from the Valley Humane Society, seemed to yearn for company, and they visited their dog's former shelter only to spot the appealing face of Petunia. The biggest question was how Brewster and Petunia might hit it off. The two were introduced in a holding pen, and the play date turned out completely idyllic. They immediately sniffed, then romped and gambled as though they had always known each other, and finally tired and lay down in peace and harmony. Petunia and Brewster now live happily with Kevin and Yvette—a model of successful adoption with people-and-dog-family happiness, and a good day for all.

The saga of these two rewarding dogs does not always represent the outcome for stray, abused, or otherwise-vagabond cats and dogs that come to the attention of the authorities, but when the stories end this way, it is a joy for God's people and animals. The Santa Ynez Valley Humane Society is a very Valley expression of our initiative and compassion and the people–animal habitation that makes us who we are. The Valley Humane Society deserves our praise and support. Check out the organization's website. You might be in for a surprise!

· **F** ·

Dog Wars

Valley people, like all homesteaders, sometimes wonder about their neighbors' choice of dog friends. Why can't everyone have a quiet, companionable dog chum, and just forget the unfriendly, aggressively territorial canine loudmouths that some folks seem to choose for household dogs?

In our immediate Alisal neighborhood, a few families share a pleasant Valley landscape with various dogs. One family makes a home for two large canines, Eddy, a friendly mix in love with the world and, unfortunately, his own voice, and an infinitely affectionate Labrador, Woody, whose eyes communicate "Love me as much as I love the world!" Next door lives a muscular Boxer named Alex who playfully drags his patient owner around the streets during a generous amount of walks. However, another family sports three large and aggressive-sounding German Shepherds that can be loud and scary to neighbors and seem more suitable for hunting werewolves in the Black Forest. Yet another family is home for two unfriendly rescue dogs, one medium in size with Pit Bull ancestors, the other a smaller troublemaker. These two are quiet at home, but a menace if let out of their compound.

This is dog-friendly country, with neighbors walking their dogs regularly up and down the streets and often becoming known more for their dogs than for who they are. Resident dogs will sometimes yowl when a walker goes by, but there is rarely any trouble. Additionally, sometimes a coyote will stealth through the paths and streets by night and early morning, but the dogs are mostly asleep then.

During their initial move-in, the German Shepherds shook the neighborhood with barks and howls, especially complaining across the fence to the neighboring Eddy and Woody, and occasionally Alex would join in the cross-fence fuss. Friendly phone calls and notes did not bring peace, so a visit from the Alisal tract committee initiated Alsatian incarceration, training, and discipline that soothed the German Shepherd racket. Neighborhood good will prevailed, and finally the bowwow settled to a normal level. But other problems arose.

One day, a neighbor lady went for a walk with the friendly Labrador on a leash, and came upon the Pit Bull and his feisty little friend who had escaped their yard. The owners were renters, one a celebrity type, who had secured the two miscellaneous dogs from a Santa Barbara County rescue facility. This celebrity lacked a sense of dog nature, however, and her well-intentioned charity did not gentrify these two bandits. At the time of the incident, the two dogs had been left with an immature house sitter who had somehow allowed them loose on the street.

The large Pit Bull type probably would have been peaceful if not for the feisty mutt, but unfortunately the small one lit out for the Lab, making loud noises that could only mean to his partner, "Come on, big boy, together we can take this stranger!"

The friendly Lab was mostly astonished by the attack, and at first let the lady lead the defense, keeping the two aggressors at bay. The two did not want to tangle with a person, but the leash became entwined, and the Lab began to fight back. Pit Bull type and small nasty circled and struck, and the noise was terrific. The battle was soon over, though, when the hapless house sitter and other neighbors rushed out to help and the two initiators slunk back to their house amid kicks and shouts.

The Lab did not seem wounded or, if he was, did not seem to mind. But the owner had been nipped slightly, and there was a trace of blood, so she walked the Lab home and cleaned up the small wound. The unfortunate incident would have ended there, except for friends who took exception to the two attackers, despite the celebrity status of their owner. The nice lady, like her friendly Lab, did not want to complain, but her indignant neighbors did not appreciate dog aggressions in the 'hood.

She was marched down to the sheriff's office, where the neighborhood complaint was officially passed on to County Animal Services. In due course, a marked truck and uniformed authority called on the aggressive dogs' home and put the fear of law, liability, and dog incarceration into the mind of the celebrity and her advisors. Happily the fighters were found clear of rabies, no one really wanted trouble, and peace once again reigned on the friendly streets. The entire celebrity household, complete with the two rescue dogs, has since relocated, and our neighborhood has returned to normal Valley dog and people tranquility.

Open warfare is a rare event on peaceful Solvang streets, but dogs will be dogs, and even Valley people have their moments. By the way, as the celebrity type has moved on, she can be known now as Carlene Carter, stepdaughter of singer Johnny Cash, and a quiet and pleasant neighbor in all things except her choice of dogs.

Part Five

COUNTRY MOMENTS

Horse Friends

One of the all-time people–animal accomplishments in our community is the Santa Ynez Valley Therapeutic Riding Program. This facility, managed by professional staff and volunteers, rests in the riding center complex, just off Refugio Road near the river. Here is a homey and somewhat-disorganized-appearing facility, housing a disparate band of good-natured horses and a mess of kid-friendly play items. Just as a nugget of pure gold rests in the Yukon River, this angel endeavor is a gem in our Valley animal life.

Certain young and old in any community are wired mentally and physically in different ways than the majority. Whether from autism spectrum disorder, cerebral injury, stress disorders due to accident or combat, or other vicissitudes of life, some of us have cognitive, learning, and behavioral difficulties daily. There are many ways of addressing these everyday problems, starting with a sympathetic understanding and generous desire from family and other supporters, but one of the best progress assists in the healthy growth toolbox is horse therapy.

What is it about horses? I once spoke with a riding instructor, trainer, and competition rider who had been working with horses all his life. This cowboy knew horses well, and admired and respected them, but confessed that after all his years he had no idea what was on their minds. Horse thoughts were a complete mystery to him. The horses at the Therapeutic Riding Program facility likewise keep their thoughts to themselves, but somewhere in their equine mind mix is the desire to work with kids and grown-ups who need their help. These blessed animals consistently maintain the attitude and patience to hold on their backs a squirming, exclaiming child or a damaged and nervous adult, and they then plod around a sand ring while working a magic of healing power.

The number of horses living at the facility varies from eight to ten, and often one will be rotated to a friendly ranch for a change of routine and scenery. Dooley is a typical therapy horse. He was retired at a mature age from the trail horse class show ring, so he was well acclimatized to people, routine, and gentle walking. He lives in a small, partially covered paddock and looks forward to his grass hay twice a day. He plays with his neighbor horses through the fence. He goes to work five days a week, where he will be groomed and saddled by staff and volunteers, and sometimes by the more advanced clients. For a treat, sometimes the horses are let out together to romp in the sand ring.

When a rider is ready, Dooley will be led to an elaborate mounting block where the rider will be mounted into the saddle, with staff and volunteers helping from both sides if necessary. A staff member or experienced volunteer will lead horse and rider to the ring, sometimes with a second side walker. Depending on the level of the rider, he will then continue from a led walk to a free walk, trot, and even canter if the rider is advanced. The session will continue from a half-hour to an hour, and Dooley then returns to the mounting block and stands quietly while the client is helped off. The sessions will continue with new clients from morning to afternoon as necessary, and the horses are all happy with the routine that they have come to understand.

A typical client might be a teenage boy with learning and behavior problems that require specialized developmental support. The boy needs help growing up, but in a different way than other kids. If the Therapeutic Riding Program becomes involved, this young man will first be brought to understand that if he earns the privilege, he will be taken to a special place and actually learn to ride a horse!

When he arrives at the friendly and no-nonsense facility, he will be greeted with trained and sympathetic instructors who will show him to the waiting area, full of toys, drums, small houses, and other intriguing activities. Gradually, he will be introduced to a horse and learn the basics of respect, quiet (as possible) behavior around his new large friend, and then how to be helped into the saddle and "ride" while being led around the sand ring with other young people on horses. The seriousness of dealing with a large animal and engaging in this demanding and intriguing activity will lead to behavior beyond the influence of any parent, teacher, counselor, or jumble of potential act-outs that the student's differentness has experienced.

One day, I observed the progress of a young boy who was known to be terrified of horses. His visit involved standing at a low rail, sheltered in the arms of a volunteer, while a small chestnut pony named Teacup was led nearby, up to other children who stroked and loved their furry friend. The pony happily accepted the attention and kind words from these more experienced children while the newcomer suspiciously eyed the beast. This went on for a time, and I detected a softening of the nervous boy's attitude. Finally, the pony was removed from the other kids, and the boy actually reached after the pony as it walked away. A knowing instructor commented, "Well, that means just one or two more sessions, and we will be riding." What might be viewed as a routine matter to most would be a huge step for that particular kid.

A horse in a therapy situation represents a demanding, but nonjudgmental, presence that requires a young individual who might otherwise mentally drift away, act up in a classroom environment, or demonstrate careless actions in home life to respond responsibly and take a small step up the ladder toward thoughtful, mature behavior. A youngster with problems will meet a situation where the desirable success of actually riding on the horse requires a heightened level of maturity and cooperation. The appeal of riding, as well as the sense of accomplishment, provides a boost in ego and a notch up toward life's normality. The well-trained instructors who guide the process do not demand calm and mature behavior for no reason because a horse is a horse. The demands and rewards of riding one present their own reality that inherently calls for a step up in thoughtful response. The Therapeutic Riding Program staff are rewarded time and time again by experiencing the progress of their clients.

A young man who is known to many of us in the Valley was diagnosed as being on the autism spectrum at an early age. His perception of reality and his different thought process caused him to act out in ways that brought difficulties at home and an inability to cope with school. His prognosis was unpromising, and even the thoughtful, sensitive, and caring efforts of his parents appeared to bring little progress.

Around the age of twelve, he had the good fortune to be sent to a boarding school in Connecticut that included a therapeutic riding program in its curriculum. The young man's response to horses was almost immediate as the potential problem child settled down with a fascination for horses and riding that stirred a positive miracle of mature behavior. When some years later the family moved to the Santa Ynez Valley, he continued his progress with our local facility and later came to be a therapeutic horse walker and instructor, working successfully with other clients. Today this friendly if somewhat other-than-usual young man works a regular job with horses at the Alisal Guest Ranch & Resort as well as regular hours in a local store. Those of us who know him understand his original wit and honesty and are charmed with his different but responsibly mature ways.

Today, facility manager Robin Serritslev and her trained staff and volunteers continue to serve around three hundred clients a week in the facility that is fully certified as one of 850 U.S. members of the Professional Association of Therapeutic Horsemanship, or PATH, International. Clients are mostly children, but also include adults and a contingent of combat veterans suffering from posttraumatic stress syndrome.

What goes on in the horse partner brains remains a mystery, but the staff know there is some animal realization of the role they are playing in the health of their riders. Often the cool-acting and knowledgeable staff need to brush back a tear when they experience the joy and progress of a happy kid growing up with these horses.

By the way, any reader who might want to support a splendid foundation in our Valley should visit the Santa Ynez Valley Therapeutic Riding Program at www.syvtherapeuticriding.org. The facility, located at 195 Refugio Road in Santa Ynez, can also be reached at (805) 598-1099, and exists with the help of contributions.

Among the many dimensions of Valley animals, this is truly one of the most rewarding. And these hardworking therapeutic horse friends dispensing their mysterious healing certainly earn their keep.

· **F** ·

Shop Talk

Carlos Quintero runs an old-fashioned barber shop in Nielsen's Marketplace Shopping Center in Solvang. He wouldn't want it labeled old-fashioned, because it is what it is, but he presides by himself, gives a superior haircut, and provides a place of gossip, confessions, boasting, and lies for local ranchers, merchants, retirees, and miscellaneous men around town. Carlos served in the U.S. Marine Corps, and his clientele tends toward the crusty, so one can imagine the drift and direction of shop philosophy.

The conversation sometimes runs loose, and often centers on Valley animal stories. One day, I happened to be sitting in the chair while a couple of grumpy locals relaxed, chatted, and waited their turn.

The silence was broken when one codger looked up from his newspaper and exclaimed, "The state of California has saved us again. Another helpful law was just passed! Starting next year, it will be a felony to eat your pets! No more dining off your family animals!"

The discussion in the shop then proceeded something like this: "How can they do this to us? What will we have for dinner?"

"You better eat up now, boy, 'cause it's lean years ahead!"

"Pretty soon we'll all be overrun with animals around the house with no use for them!"

"What will I do with my freezer full of lovables?"

"All those damn songbirds my wife has been keeping will go to waste!"

Despite suppressed guffaws, Carlos only missed a couple of snips, but he soldiered on with my haircut among the wisecracks resonating in his shop. He did mumble something about banning newspapers from now on.

The wit and wisdom continued. "Even if we invite all our friends, I doubt if I can get through all the ranch dogs before next year."

"Your Christmas dinner will be a treat!"

"I've got the solution—we'll take the pack to Arizona and enjoy 'em there!"

"Brilliant! Raise pets in California and consume 'em in Arizona. That'll show those damn Sacramento lawmakers!"

Finally the subject died off, and I slipped out of the chair, a neater and more presentable package after Carlos's ministrations. When I reached the truck, my loyal Shepherd dog, Tucker, gave me the once over. He took a second questioning look, and something in his face seemed to say, "I know you have been up to something, but I don't know what."

Prayerful Creatures

There are a number of vital churches in the Valley. Most locals have an affiliation with one of the religious communities, and it is usual and expected to be so identified, despite the modern trends of secularization and competing activities in the world beyond the Valley. St. Mark's-in-the-Valley Episcopal Church in Los Olivos is both a worship center and a meeting place for organizations and tourists alike. Animals also play their part in St. Mark's life.

A hint of St. Mark's creature commitment is a permanent and freshly maintained dog water station. Another symbol is the endearing and proprietary presence of Ike, the white Bichon Frisé who is the charming dog friend of the rector, Randall Day, and his partner, Billy Hurbaugh. Ike joined their family from the Poodle Rescue Network of Southern California and is a wandering, unleashed personality attending most services and events at St. Mark's. He is carried to the Communion rail, meanders among the pews during services, and sometimes perches on a chair in the singers' section during choir rehearsals. His regular attendance symbolizes the church's commitment to dog inclusion.

Once, during after-service coffee hour, a stranger noted the smiling and welcoming Ike strolling amongst the parishioners. The visitor commented, "It is wonderful that you welcome dogs into your church services."

"Yes," replied the local, "and we very much do so, but you must know that Ike is not really a dog!"

Barbara Brown's miniature Yorkshire Terrier, Sam—alas, no longer with us—used to pace the choir and look at Mom longingly, asking when it would be time to go home, while our Miniature American Shepherd,

Chelsea, often attends choir rehearsal and peacefully dozes, seemingly enjoying our singing efforts. Similarly, our choir director's sons, Michael and William, love to bring their Shih Tzu puppy, Wendel, to choir rehearsal. But this bundle of affectionate energy has a very limited attention span. Sometimes the small, gray presence joins the Sunday school group and demonstrates a small-dog character, long on love but short on quiet meditation.

Jessica Schley and her mother, Teona Schley, bring their large female hunting hound, Taio, to services. Taio has no use for hunting, but her abiding love and curiosity regarding humans shows itself in a searching nose and soulful gaze encompassing all around her. At the Communion rail, she will stand with her front feet on the kneeling cushions and closely watch all the people crouched around her. Taio's expression of love and longing for the greater spiritual world is plain for all to see.

The highlight of the St. Mark's creatures' church year is the Blessing of the Animals service that takes place on St. Francis's Sunday afternoon, on the church lawn. Cats, rabbits, canaries, turtles, and of course a plethora of dogs show up for a late-afternoon service and blessing. Sometimes even horses, goats, and alpacas join the crowd, carefully tethered to their sponsors, eyeing each other, and wondering in their creature way what this is all about. Dog personalities are very much revealed as some curl up at their owner's feet and doze, some express irresistible curiosity about their neighbors, and one or two inevitably break loose to inspire confusion. Most just resign themselves peacefully to this harmless people thing.

The animal Sunday service proceeds with prayers, psalms, a reading from St. Francis, a reading from Dostoevsky, and welcome words from the rector, Randall Day. The highlight occurs when the good rector passes through the assembled crowd of animals with a hands-on blessing and comfortable words for each, while in the background the splendid voice of Adam Phillips sings folk music. The forty to fifty congregation animals receive their blessing as Father Randall walks on in the spirit of St. Francis and wiping traces of grateful dog lick.

Our neighbors, Don and Susan Krog, once brought their large and energetic Boxer, Alex. This magnificent specimen received his moment of blessing with Boxer dignity. A few animals along from Alex, Mark Herthel had brought his own young family and their beloved rabbits. After the Boxer's moment of blessing, the large dog belly-crept along on the grass, straining his heavy leash, staring longingly at the bunnies in their cage. A fixed gaze and signs of drool on his chops betrayed his innermost thoughts to be no less than "Rabbit pie for dinner!" We all want to be better creatures, but the hungry Boxer reminded us that we are all also sinners.

The good Lord is chuckling!

Senior Stalls

Local resident C. C. Beaudette-Wellman might be a poster child for people–animal relationships in the Santa Ynez Valley. Daughter of the glamorous Cobina Wright, a famous actress and socialite who at one time lived in the Valley, C. C. attended Dunn School and learned her love of horses, and also acquired a dedication to the rescue and well-being of animals. After her own career as a model and actress, she finally moved back to Santa Ynez, and lives—now by herself, except for ten aged and debilitated horses, the maximum allowed by Santa Barbara County zoning—on a ten-acre property.

Advanced age brings physical problems to people that sometimes require a retirement home or other assisted living. Many simply lose physical and mental capacity in senior years and cannot live alone. Such was the case with a well-known and very able local Western competition rider of a certain age. He had reached the point of needing assisted living, and his family and friends helped him into a local retirement facility. He was happy and secure with the arrangement, but a problem arose because his last champion horse, named Tucker, that he had not ridden in some time but had fed and looked after, would now be abandoned, without care and housing.

This aged though still very much alive horse boasted many trail event and horse show competition trophies and had carried his now-retired boss for many ranch workdays. Tucker was well known to friends and Valley riders, but his sagging back had borne a last saddle, and he had been in retirement, attended to by his boss, for a few years. Assisted care facilities are very much available for aging people, but not so much for aging horses.

Fortunately in Tucker's case, the community had befriended the horse and found the perfect solution, securing him a place at C. C.'s Happy Endings Animal Sanctuary. Now, several years later, the black horse—whose muzzle and coat are flecked with gray, whose bowed back is very much different from his glory days, and whose legs look more like mature grapevines than stellar show ring conformation—is a contented retiree.

His slow, easy shuffle as he meanders around his retirement paddock and his friendly and benign attitude demonstrate a happy horse, content with C. C.'s care and concern.

On her ten-acre hillside, C. C. rescues castaway or otherwise-needy older horses or those like Tucker who are brought to her attention. The county authorities and the cowboy and riding community know of her and know that, if they can place an abandoned or ailing horse with her, the animal will be lucky and well kept. These animals-in-need are cared for permanently, with volunteers supervised by C. C. and through her foundation that is dedicated to their welfare. The ten retired boarders shuffle quietly about the paddocks, communicating with each other and the occasional people staff or visitor, and wait for the two high points of the day: feeding time.

Since 2007, Happy Endings has supplied shelter, feed, dental and veterinary care, and loving attention to ten horses, the most that are allowed on C. C.'s property, who are content to spend their aged, slow-motion days in safety and security. Her neighbors think she is a little balmy, but are supportive, and her volunteers are dedicated and love their work. Schoolchildren are regularly brought by the property to learn horse care and concern for all animals.

A few cats and dogs and even a homeless peacock have somehow found their way to shelter as well, because the facility has a big heart. But C. C.'s program is for horses. While some of the students who visit the facility grow up to be volunteers, all of them grow by the example of C. C.'s animal love and dedication.

The bright lights of Hollywood may be a past memory for C. C., but her beacon of caring shines brilliantly in our Valley.

· **F** ·

Bad Actors

Solvang is rightly proud of its Theaterfest, the beautiful outdoor Festival Theater that hosts splendid performances by PCPA—Pacific Conservatory Theatre as well as many community and traveling shows and events. Locals enjoy continuing amusement watching tourists enter the evening shows dressed in their summer wear, only to later learn the hard way that our Pacific Ocean climate resembles an ice age when the sun goes down. A blanket concession at the entrance then does a booming trade. In addition to fresh air and stars overhead, our country setting often treats tourists to a guest appearance from our Valley animal friends.

In the Santa Ynez Valley, theater entertainment is often shared with a population of Valley critters who also enjoy the shows. Some animals live in the structure, some pass through by accident, and some make their homes in the great trees that surround the theater. None of these creatures buy a ticket, and locals and performers have learned to expect anything from the animal kingdom.

When the dark settles in, the resident bats zoom across the stage, over the audience, and occasionally, like night bombers in searchlights, are illuminated or at least shadowed to bring gasps from the uninitiated. These night flyers are quite harmless and silent, except on the rare occasion when they are not. A disoriented bat once landed on Sarah Lambie Greenman's formal dress in the middle of My Fair Lady. To her great credit and thanks to her experience with the local wildlife hazards, the intrepid actress did not miss a beat.

The best of all bat stories occurred one night when Count Dracula stood at the top of a ten-foot staircase about to turn into a bat and flee the castle. A mechanical pulley system that would appear to fly him transformed into a bat, over the audience, simulating the escape of the count. On this one night, miraculously, a real bat flew out from backstage produced fog, and circled the audience before exiting to the night. The startled patrons gave the bat actor a round of applause, and the production continued on cue with actors, crew, and audience amazed by the unscripted realism.

Pigeons are occasionally wakened from their nests and soar over the stage. These messy visitors often leave a white splotch calling card for the actors to ignore on the stage. During one evening performance of The Last Night of Ballyhoo, actress Polly Firestone Walker was scripted to hand off a cup of coffee to a fellow actress, only to discover it was liberally decorated by a passing pigeon. The coffee prop was fortunately obscured from the audience, and the actors did not even consider simulating the drinking.

One recent season, a huge pair of owls made their nest in a giant elm tree that graces the sky over the theater. The nightly call of these lover birds became important because the "huu HOO hooo hoooo" song of the common local great horned owl was heard by an official of the California Department of Fish and Wildlife to perhaps be the "huup hoo hoo hooo" of the endangered and highly protected spotted owl. If the theater bird visitors were truly the latter, and if anyone from the Theaterfest cast or staff so much as shook the tree, someone might spend time in prison for violating an endangered species.

The owl family remained in their high nest above the theater, and that season, newly hatched young owlets made a dramatic theatrical debut. One showtime evening, actress Kerry Neal sang "Have Yourself a Merry Little Christmas" in the play The 1940's Radio Hour. For some mystical show business reason, at that singing moment, the owl family chicks woke up and cheeped an audible squawking in a syncopated rhythm that the actress could not hear but the audience could clearly follow. Equally strangely, the chicks quieted when the song finished, and the audience burst into applause for both soloist and owl chorus. Actor Ben Bottoms was Kerry Neal's partner, and as he exited with her, he ad-libbed the words, "But if you're going to keep those partridges in the number, you're going to need to teach them how to find their pitch." Both the audience and the actors on stage lost their composure in howls of laughter.

A dramatic entrance was staged by a mother opossum with at least three babies in tow who crossed the set during a performance of Heart's Desire. Leo Cortez acted a part that called for him to lie dead on the stage directly in the opossum path. He saw the procession approaching and just closed his eyes and hoped for the best. Fortunately, mother opossum and family exited without passing over him, but with gasps from the audience. Another night, an opossum scurried across the stage and hid in the scenery during a performance of Twelfth Night. In historic Globe Theatre tradition, neither audience nor actors broke their concentration, and the show continued as though there was nothing to see.

A favorite actress, Kitty Balay, once opened the play You Can't Take It with You with a young kitten on her typewriter, which she was to put in a cage and hand off to another, unfortunately inexperienced, actor. Over the weeks the play ran, the kitten grew and became more rambunctious with every performance. Finally, the scene-stealing kitty cat opened the play by jumping off the typewriter and under a couch on the set. The green handoff actor lost her composure and stood mouth-open amazed with an empty cage. However, veteran Kitty Balay continued her dialogue as fellow actors entered, casually ad-libbing their lines and movements while she circled and searched under the sofa. The play continued, and luckily the kitten decided to bolt for the wing and into the arms of stage hands . . . but not without applause from the audience.

The Theaterfest use of stage animals is the amusing, reassuring, and homey sharing of our Valley theater experience with our Valley animal friends, even though none of these animal actors would ever pass up an audition on Broadway. Unlike the exotic camels and whitewashed horses in grand Italian operas, adding a presence to splendid productions, our local animals at Theaterfest are homebodies, and just part of our lives.

The movie of Steinbeck's Of Mice and Men, starring Gary Sinise and John Malkovich, was partly made in our Valley in the 1990s. Tom LePley and a number of local horsey characters were hired as extras to film the sheriff's chase scene and other backgrounds. Tom remembers the professional actor dog brought in to film the sad scene where the debilitated, old animal was taken out to be put down, much to the sorrow of Malkovich's tragic character, Lennie Small.

When the same story was presented as a play at Theaterfest, the local producers did not have the budget for a trained acting dog and decided to use J.D., a friendly white Samoyed owned by Polly Firestone Walker, who acted a part in the play. A problem developed when Polly's energetic J.D. appeared too lively to be a sick dog needing sympathetic euthanasia, but the PCPA cast members were up to the problem. After careful consultation, a mild veterinarian's sedative was administered, and the dog settled into her part very convincingly.

On stage, J.D. was perfect in the scene, with slow, hesitant movements and a plaintive look on her face as she was carried offstage to be put down. During that sad exit, many of us who knew Polly and her lovable dog were sobbing in the audience, while the dog herself, slightly zonked, thoroughly enjoyed her starring role.

Samoyeds are known to be intelligent, and this lady dog was clearly at the top of her class. As rehearsals and then the run of the play continued, J.D. seemed to understand the part and developed a sadly sympathetic demeanor that brought agony to actors, stage crew, and audience. When the failing dog was carried out to be killed, there were even growls from the audience at such cruelty. Locals who knew Polly and the pet were very pleased the first-time actor's doggy debut was such a hit.

Our Valley Theaterfest is a great source of delight, and locals and tourists happily enjoy the playacting, planned and unplanned, of local animals. May our Valley show animals always go on.

Deputy Dogs

Among our Valley animal friends are a few who are chosen to serve and protect us. The Santa Barbara County Sheriff's Office maintains four highly trained and capable K9 duty dogs—three to track and subdue, and one a specialized sniffer. All these dogs live and work with their handlers, providing a valuable dimension to our law enforcement capability.

The Valley and the ugly, outside world of crime clashed in 2017, when a counterfeit crook visited one of our Solvang tasting rooms and attempted to purchase a genuine beautiful Valley wine with a bogus hundred-dollar bill. The wine facility featured a new bill tester next to the cash register, and when the server ran the bill, it turned up counterfeit. In no time the busted crook was out the door, and the server was on the phone to 911 reporting the crime. An on-duty sheriff's car was dispatched to the scene, but it happened that a K9 unit was patrolling the Valley and first to arrive.

The deputy quickly learned that the bad guy did not escape in a vehicle, but had run across the road and disappeared down a steep ravine behind a motel at the western edge of town. Deputy Mike McNeal and his partner, an experienced and ferocious German Shepherd tracker dog named Betty, arrived and summed up the situation. Betty was unleashed and soon found the fugitive's scent down the thickly brushed arroyo.

All dogs sport the capability of finding and discerning scents beyond our imagination. For instance, they do not smell just a ham sandwich, but identify the bread, lettuce, mayonnaise, ham, pickle, and mustard separately and understand subtle differences in the strength and background of each individual ingredient. In this case, the fleeing suspect's scent was fresh and available, and Betty was on the trail, into the brush.

Soon Deputy McNeal heard Betty's loud and distinctive bark, but was unable to see the action hidden in the foliage. He called to his deputy dog partner, and Betty was calling back urgently. Finally, McNeal made his way to the capture scene to find Betty standing on the chest of the offender, who had tried to hide, but now was very much willing to give up. An Alsatian bark inches from one's face is a great equalizer, and the crook needed little persuasion to surrender to the handcuffs.

German Shepherds, as the Alsatians are known in the Americas, were originally bred for herding sheep, but their strength, trainability, and obedience makes them preferred candidates for search and rescue, police, and military work around the world. They are trained by professionals from an early age, and the graduates are purchased by law enforcement departments and matched with permanent handlers who come to know and love their dog partners. Their service is a valuable tool in the law enforcement field, and our Santa Barbara sheriffs make good use of these essential deputy dogs.

In searching for Valley animal stories, I learned of the Solvang capture, and visited a K9 training session. I did not meet Betty, but became acquainted with a huge and ferocious-looking partner of hers named Magnum who was on training duty that day. I asked if we could reenact the capture, and at first the deputies were reluctant to put an innocent animal story writer who had passed no bad bills in harm's way. At last they relented, I lay down, and the obedient and willing monster dog stood on my chest, looking into my eyes (as pictured on the cover). If ever I had a yen to go bad, I assured Magnum that I was now on the straight and narrow.

Later in the demonstration, I was allowed to secrete a bag of marijuana in my coat pocket and casually sit on the floor against a wall in a room full of deputies and observers. An enthusiastic dog partner, in this case a Labrador named Crypto, was let loose and told to find. The energetic Lab ran around the room a few times, sniffing out the company, and in no time sat down beside me with a satisfied and knowing dog grin. I was busted, and the deputy partner praised and played with Crypto as a reward.

When dogs are on the scene, dope dealers know an arrest will soon follow. Deputy Heather Van Hemert and her Labrador partner were recently called in to search a suspect car full of clothes and trash, but possibly a dealer's wares. Her sniffer dog partner rummaged through the messy vehicle interior without much luck, except with a bucket of trail mix, in which she buried her nose with interest. Another time she had come up with a full, round, moldy, old pizza in a search instead of contraband, and Deputy Van Hemert was suspicious that her always-hungry partner was enjoying the mix and not the investigation. But the deputy dog persisted, and on digging into the bucket, a dealer's quantity packet of heroin was discovered that earned the driver a trip to the county jail.

The current four Santa Barbara County dogs have been trained and purchased for thousands of dollars by our Sheriff's Office. Not all dogs can handle the extensive schooling, but the bright animals who take to the training then must be willing to do what they have learned consistently and obediently. The Alsatians have a potent weapon in their bite, and just as with a pistol sidearm, the weapon must be used judiciously and sparingly. The dogs are trained to chase, neutralize, and bark at a fleeing suspect, but never to bite unless they are instructed to do so. In the training session, a "suspect" is poised with a heavily protected arm guard, and on command, the loosed partner dog will corner and then bark only, withholding the bite unless commanded. It is an impressive sight.

In 2016, a suspect's car fled a crime scene from neighboring San Luis

Obispo County and sped down Highway 101, reaching speeds, clocked by the chasing patrol cars, of over one hundred miles per hour. The fugitive raced through Santa Maria, and the chase was turned over to the California Highway Patrol and also a hovering helicopter. Tire-bursting strips were placed on the highway at the junction of 101 and 154, and the bad guy's car was brought to a halt north of Buellton. Here a standoff shut the highway down.

An individual, assessed to be under the influence of drugs, was holed up in the vehicle, and the CHP officer was worried that the man was armed. The suspect would open his pickup truck door occasionally, but not come out to surrender, and appeared highly threatening to the officers and even suicidal. The standoff continued, and the man could not be talked out, nor could the officers approach this bad-acting individual.

Fortunately, Deputy McNeal and Magnum were in the area and called to the scene. McNeal approached from the rear with his partner poised as the CHP officer and fugitive called back and forth. Finally, the driver opened his door, and Magnum lunged, just in time to enter and seize the deranged man's arm. The pickup window was open, however, and Magnum jumped in, biting an arm and beginning a heroic fight. Only after McNeal and the highway patrolman wrestled the driver out and onto the ground, with Magnum biting the other arm, would the drugged-up fugitive give in. This arrest demonstrated the true law enforcement partnership of dog and deputy.

Valley residents should respect and admire these Valley animal law enforcement partners, but petting is not advised.

Animal Responders

Our sheriff's deputies and firefighters train long and hard for every conceivable circumstance, but often there is no manual of procedure for the curves thrown their way by our Valley animals. The state and county wildlife services people are not always immediately available for four-footed threats and emergencies, and the quick thinking and country backgrounds of our deputies and firefighters are a gift to us all. Here are some scenes from our first responders.

When a trailer full of horses overturned on San Marcos Pass, the sheriffs were first on the scene of the wreck. Deputy Brian Thielst remembers well the deputies having to corral the loose horses and deal with the others in the overturned trailer. One animal was pulled out and hoisted into a horse ambulance from Dr. Herthel's clinic. Others were pulled out and bandaged, but one sadly too far gone was euthanized. The incident could have been much worse without the deputies' quick thinking and action.

Deputy Matthew McFarlin recalls a threat from a mountain lion wandering on the fringe of a county park. In this instance, he and his partner swelled themselves up, waved their arms, and shouted at the big cat. After a brief summing up, the lion was last seen hightailing back to the mountains with a notion that people were crazy and best avoided. The deputies, of course, had their hands on their pistols.

Another call came in from a motorist who had noticed a cow in distress just off a county road. Deputy Sandra Rivera responded, and fortunately, she had grown up on a ranch. The cow was down and calving, but the calf was stuck, and both mother and baby had limited survival prospects if something was not done quickly. A volunteer country man offered to help, a number of motorists stopped and stared, and a small herd of seemingly sympathetic cows gathered and gazed helplessly as the drama played out and Deputy Rivera went into action.

While the man held the cow's head, the good deputy rolled up her sleeves and grabbed the calf's feet sticking just out of the mother cow's birth canal. There was no time for niceties, and the cow just seemed to accept without a struggle that man and deputy meant well. The motorist crowd and bovine herd watched as the tugging match progressed and the messy, reluctant calf was extracted. The calf staggered to its feet, and the cow rose and began licking her newborn. The crowd cheered, and Deputy Rivera wiped off the slime, recovered her dignity, and drove off for a shower. There was no code in the law enforcement book to call in for this incident.

Bears wander into backyards and campgrounds seeking nourishment, and back-country fires will drive bear families into civilization to escape the flames. Often deputies will be called to chase the furry culprits or at least protect people until animal control can arrive with darts that will bring sleep and relocation. A strange bear encounter occurred when Sergeant Kelly Hoover was dispatched to a preschool facility that was celebrating, of all things, a "Teddy Bear's Picnic." While the kids' picnic was proceeding on the grass, an actual black bear appeared in the bushes behind the school. The screams, lockdown, and deputies were adequate to drive the bear back to the hills, unfortunately missing the picnic.

Aggressive dogs are a continual challenge to our sheriffs. Deputy Christopher MacAuley had a moment of truth when he was called to investigate a suspicious character lurking near the Chumash reservation. He arrived to find a not-so-innocent-looking individual with a very large, ugly dog on a stout leash, and the pair obviously out of place. The man did not want to be questioned, and could not be approached with the snarling Pit Bull ready to fight. Deputy MacAuley walked toward the man, but the dog lunged, just held back by the leash. The solution was to secure a cable around a tree and require the man to tie the dog out of harm's way.

As the sheriff opened his car for a cable, his keys fell to the ground, and he bent down to pick them up. He had kept his watch on the threatening Pit Bull, and now was on eye level with the dog. This confrontation caused the raving animal to charge with all his might, breaking away from the leash hold restraint. Sheriff's training kicked in, and a saving side-step duck caused the killer dog to miss the deputy on his first pass, but the Pit Bull rolled around and scrambled for another lethal lunge. Training again saved the day, and the legendary Marshal Wyatt Earp would have been proud of Deputy MacAuley's two deadly shots that dropped the killer dog dead.

By now the sheriff's backup had arrived who radioed out the words that always incite sirens and action: "Shots fired!" By the time the dust had settled, the handcuffed outlaw was found to have a fortune in drugs available for sale and was on his way to jail. On investigation, it was also revealed that the heavy-duty guard dog was a known bad actor used for protection at a Hells Angels chapter. The deputy was congratulated for quick, cool, and effective action.

Deputy Thomas Jenkins was on a more or less routine assignment to serve a warrant and bring in a suspect. He drove to a rural house, and as he approached the front door, a snarling, angry guard dog came hurling toward him. The dog paused for a moment, and the two had a standoff until a second   threatening partner came dashing around the corner of the house. The two potentially lethal dogs paused, growled, separated, and began closing in slowly on each side of the sheriff in true hunter-killer style.

Deputy Jenkins did not want to shoot his pistol, so he pulled out his pepper spray canister. His first shot caught the closest dog straight to the face, which caused it to sit back in pain and confusion. The second dog paused to discover what was up with his partner, and Deputy Jenkins caught the second, also straight to the head. The two fighters retreated, completely whipped, back around the house in dog tears. But when the deputy knocked on the door, the occupant had fled from the back, and the warrant could not be served.

A couple of days later, Deputy Jenkins returned to renew his arrest, and once again knocked on the house door. The two vicious dogs once again came rushing from the back of the house, but this time they both stopped in their tracks and slunk back out of sight with a "nothing here to see!" expression. When the suspect opened the door, he was immediately cuffed and marched out to the squad car. Finally, he had to ask, "Where are my dogs?"

"Oh, my two new friends?" Deputy Jenkins replied happily. "They just said hello and went back to sleep!"

As in most communities, the Fire Department is the source of animal rescue stories, but here in the Valley, the furry population seems to be able to take care of itself, and our local firefighters lacked stories. It seems that they are seldom called upon to effect rescues and have little interaction with Valley animals.

One local first responder did have a shaggy cat story to share. The classic firefighter rescue is the stranded cat who has wandered to some threatening height and is unable to descend, and sure enough, our locals were called upon by a distressed lady who had spotted a cat high in a tree, obviously stuck and stranded. Our heroes responded with truck and ladder, and one gloved athlete ascended high, but returned empty-handed.

"Where's the kitty?" asked the concerned citizen.

"Lady, that's no house cat," the fireman replied. "That's a bobcat, and as far as I am concerned, it's on its own!"

The fire truck returned to the station, the lady returned to good intentions, and the bobcat retreat is unrecorded.

Freshman Lecture

Rancheros Visitadores is a venerable riding fraternity that meets once a year in the hills above the Valley. Over a thousand members rendezvous with their horses for a week to ride and sit around the campfire to catch up with each other amongst great friendship and camaraderie. Every year, some thirty new men, known as Mavericks, are invited to seek membership.

A maverick on a Western ranch is an unbranded calf, often motherless, who is looking for a home. Among the numerous applicants for Rancheros membership, a committee selects those most likely to fit in and survive a first year, which includes some harassment, and then enjoy a long happy life in this unique group.

Rancheros is a special family, and bringing the new class of Mavericks into the herd is a time-honored process, involving serious learning of traditions, lore, and the parameters of membership. The new-member pastimes also include a little harmless jostling and practical joking, with gags ranging from simple fun to elaborate theater.

On the first morning of the week's activities, as the regular members arrive at camp, the new entries are required to sit through a series of talks about history, traditions, rules of conduct, expectations, and so on presented by older members who not only know what they are talking about but can also hold the attention of dozy Mavericks. The sessions go on for a full morning. One year, by prior arrangement and special dispensation from the board of directors, a well-conceived and staged, and very different, lecture took place, and the perpetrators pretty much got away with the act.

After hearing about the history of Rancheros, the many traditions, expected behavior, horse and Maverick health, and various other serious and necessary topics, the "Committee for the Ethical Disposal of Horses" was introduced.

Five carefully rehearsed members filed on to the lecture stage and proceeded to outline the following arrangements for expired horses:

First, a veterinarian gave a talk about the stressful atmosphere for horses on the Rancheros ride. With medical precision, he outlined the arduous trails, exhaustion, many strange horses on the picket line, the noisy camp environment, unfamiliar feed, heat, and other unhealthy, life-threatening conditions. He explained that even experienced horses have problems with these circumstances, and particularly new members' horses often succumb in the first year. The expectation was that a few Mavericks' horses would expire, and he was sorry, but that was the Rancheros experience. Fortunately, the Rancheros organization had evolved a productive system for dealing with the dead.

The next "committee member" explained the use of yellow ear tags, which had been printed and were passed out to each now very attentive Maverick. When a horse dies, the tack should be removed and placed by the side of the trail to be picked up by following vehicles. Then, the yellow tag with the Ranchero's name and address should be firmly fixed to the expired horse's ear. Soon another staff truck would come by to bring the horseless Ranchero to camp, and a second truck would follow to secure the horse remains. Of course, if the horse died in camp, as often happens, the process would be somewhat easier.

Another "committee member" was a certified public accountant, and passed out carefully counterfeited Internal Revenue Service (IRS) forms. He explained that the horse carcass removed from the trail or picket line by Rancheros staff is immediately taken to a rendering plant where the flesh is butchered, cooked, and canned for shipment to France. The canned meat is handled by a foundation designed to supplement the culinary supplies of orphanages in France, where horsemeat on the table is normal and appreciated. Because the foundation is registered in the United States, the member whose horse expires will receive a copy of the IRS form, fully

completed, with the "donation" able to be calculated as a charitable, fully deductible contribution.

Each lecture segment had been carefully rehearsed and was delivered with the same intensity as the history of Rancheros and other lectures. The "committee" held a serious demeanor and never cracked a grin through the entire presentation. The old hands who were in on the gag kept set expressions, and other members and staff in attendance wondered what the hell was going on, but knew enough also to keep their composure.

At this point, the "committee chair" explained that this year the Rancheros were honored to have the French president of the foundation as a guest. A venerable Ranchero of Basque extraction, Lucien Escalier (who, alas, is no longer with us), dressed in a business suit with a European air, stepped forward to express his great thanks. In fluent French, translated by the so-called committee chair, he thanked the organization profusely for many years of shipping valuable horsemeat to the orphanages of France, and went on to hope that the new members would continue the generous tradition.

So far, the "committee" was winning. The Mavericks sat in rapt and somewhat nonplussed attention, privately wondering if their horses would survive. The atmosphere was serious and even somewhat somber. Then, like many winners, the "committee" almost went too far.

The last point to be made was that occasionally Rancheros have been known to totally lose patience with their horses. Those that jig, fret, prance, and sometimes kick other horses on the trail can make men lose patience. These animals make their riders miserable, and are also a cause for extreme discomfort and shame. Some Rancheros then refuse to take those horses home; some never ever want to see them again. Here, printed red tags were passed out to the Mavericks. This system was simply to tie the horse by the side of the trail, or at the end of the day to the end of the picket line, with the red tag affixed to an ear. The horse would be picked up and humanely put down, and the owner, once again, would receive the full value of the horsemeat contribution. The "committee" assured the Mavericks that this would be done in an ethical and painless manner.

The act was still a winner! The "committee" and "foundation chair" received polite applause from the Mavericks, as accorded to all the speakers, and filed out of the meeting area with solemn demeanor. The Mavericks, clutching their tags and forms, spoke a worried murmur among themselves, as they never thought about putting their prized horses to such risks. The old hands attending the meeting never gave away so much as a smirk. The gag had been swallowed whole, and the Mavericks were left to gradually realize in the days ahead that they had been had.

The "Ethical Disposal of Horses" gang then prepared for a cold one and a congratulatory guffaw on an act well carried out. Certainly, most psychiatric therapists would agree that occasionally acting like a lunatic is a boon to mental health.

By the way, the Rancheros Visitadores have multiple veterinarians in attendance and hardly ever lose either horses or members during the week, except to unavoidable old age.

· **F** ·

Club Confusion

The following vignette does not have anything to do with animals, but has much to do with the Valley.

Back in 1972, when Kate and I were contemplating moving from London to the Santa Ynez Valley, we booked a week at the Alisal Guest Ranch & Resort to stay with our family and get a sense of what life would be like in this area, new to us. The week went well, and we decided to move. We knew some local people and asked around to find out as much as we could about the area. I cannot remember precisely where I learned this story, but I also heard it confirmed, and believe it to be true. What it says about the Valley was important to us and deserves to be told.

Although two and a half hours from Hollywood, the Santa Ynez Valley had not become an area frequented by people connected with the movie industry. However, Dean Martin, famous for his singing and also a number of film hits, learned about a home available just off the Santa Ynez River that caught his imagination. In the late 1960s, the Palacio del Rio was the grandest establishment here, owned by Jack Mitchell, a substantial business type and founder of Los Rancheros Visitadores. He had decided to sell, and Martin wanted the beautiful house.

Martin was a famous and avid golfer, and accordingly, someone put him up for membership in the Alisal golf club, at that time the only golf course in the Valley. Unfortunately, Martin showed up to play unannounced, before he was made a member of the club, perhaps just assuming he would be wanted as a member due to his notoriety. He played his round, but the membership committee took exception to his behavior and turned down his application. Martin took a dim view of the locals' decision, dropped his offer to buy the Palacio, and moved on.

When we heard that story, we felt very positive about moving to the Valley. We were not avid golfers, and would not be applying for golf club membership, but we very much liked the attitude of the committee.

· 🅕 ·

Bird Drop

Our Valley raptors, fierce birds of prey, tour the skies or perch on trees, wires, and poles eyeballing the land and searching for lunch. Food comes in many scampering forms from squirrels and rabbits to mice, rats, and maybe a larger animal that has fallen on hard times. Most dramatically, a hawk will occasionally seize a snake, fond of dozing in the sun and never suspecting a threat from the sky. The struggle of reptile and bird is then one of the rare, startling, and dreadfully dramatic sights in the Valley.

In my nearly fifty years here, I have only witnessed one such bird–snake encounter while riding on the ranch, and it was an amazing scene. The hawk had seized a snake, probably a rattler, and I first spied the two in the air, a dramatic sight with one coiling and twisting, the other frantically flapping wings to gain height for the lethal drop. All of this was silhouetted in a cloudless blue-sky background of peace and tranquility.

Finally, from a couple hundred feet, the bird dropped the snake, who then hit the ground hard enough to expire and provide a bird dinner. I watched from horseback as the big bird landed and carried off the dead snake, flapping wings hard to handle the weight. The scene was typical of a bird–snake encounter, with seizure, desperate flight, squirming thrash to escape, and the final drop to death—a rare link in the food chain, and certainly the definition of the saying, "If you snooze, you lose."

The sight I witnessed was so bizarre and startling that it is hard to describe, and may be hard to believe unless one has actually observed such a struggle high in the air. One might think that the snake could simply strike the bird, but of course the reptile might realize a bite could disable the bird, and that wings were essential for survival with the ground a long way down. Once the hawk had the snake in the air, the outcome was a sure thing.

A local was peacefully doing garden work in his backyard one sunny Saturday afternoon in the Jonata Springs Ranch area north of Buellton. As he was bent over in work, he heard a sudden crash on a pile of wood behind the house. When he investigated the sound, he saw a large, six-button rattlesnake laid out dead on the wood. He heard a thrashing and, on looking up, saw a hawk hovering, but not anxious to swoop down near the man and snatch up his lunch.

The big hawk and the man eyed each other for a moment, until the man decided his project could wait and walked in the house to let the bird fly away with lunch. The snake was dead, and somehow the hawk was shy about approaching the house. The snake was finally shoveled into some further backyard bushes, and the next day it had vanished, hopefully to a hardworking hawk.

The gardening chore had turned into a rare and brutal Valley struggle. Later, in telling the story, the man could hardly believe the encounter himself, but, in fact, a dead-to-rights Valley animal drama dropped from the sky had played out in his peaceful yard.

· 🅕 ·

Bunny Rescue

As of this writing, in the summer of 2020, a personable but aggressive and territorial crow population is very much in evidence at the Alisal Guest Ranch & Resort. The birds sit high in the trees, eyeballing us folks below; soar the skies; and croak in their crow way mornings and evenings. We never know what they are saying, but it probably is not complimentary. There is some concern that the intelligent and large birds are replacing many of our smaller songbirds, but that is the way of nature.

Crows need to eat, and this led to a food chain scene that is not appealing to animal lovers—certainly not to the Ballantine family whose home trees are a regular stopover for the flying crow population.

One day, Davey Ballantine, the mature visiting family son, walked out into the garden to discover an animal drama that needed intervention. A hungry crow had seized on a baby bunny and was just in the process of pecking the little one into a stew. Fortunately, the butchery had only begun, and Davey waved the big, black bird back to the high trees where the crow gave back the evil eye. The bunny was alive, but pecked, traumatized, and looking for help.

Davey's mother, Molly, held the bloodied bunny in her hand and, with the patient wrapped in kitchen towels, spoke loving words. Soon she made life-giving cleanups and brought reassurance to a surrendering and grateful young rabbit. The restorative drama played out over the dinner hour while the little creature buried itself in the basket blankets and settled in for the night. The next morning, a refreshed rabbit child munched on the carrots and lettuce set out in the basket, and on the sunny day, the small, grateful bunny was let loose in the grass, and proceeded to bushes, hopefully to another waiting family, and well away from hungry crows.

This little drama well illustrates the interaction between Valley families and the harsh facts of nature. Local types grasp and understand the realities of our Valley animal food chain, but also bring their loving sympathy and helpfulness to that understanding. We celebrate, but likewise comprehend, this natural course of life in our pleasant country— very much set apart from fantasyland Disney cartoon stories on one side, and from an uncaring savage jungle on the dark side of animal life.

Pandemic Paws

As this book of Valley animals episodes is being composed, the country is beset with the historic COVID-19 pandemic. The outcome, as of this writing, is still in doubt, but the response of the Valley is complete, intelligent, and effective. People are taking every advised precaution and being respectful of each other. Social distancing is the norm, and those of us who are in jeopardy are carefully sheltering in home quarantine. Additionally, as might be expected from the locals, our Valley pets are being helped through the bad days, and the C.A.R.E.4Paws organization is in the forefront.

All too often in normal times, there are people situations that place our animal friends in distress, even through innocent bystanders. For example, a situation of domestic violence may result in a battered spouse rescued by a sheriff's deputy or county welfare authorities. The family will be separated and sheltered, housed, or otherwise protected and possibly the offender jailed, but there may well be a family pet caught in the middle and threatened. Whom do you call? C.A.R.E.4Paws is the organization that comes to the rescue of such an animal. C.A.R.E. stands for community awareness, responsibility, and education, and the Paws part represents, of course, our furry household friends.

C.A.R.E.4Paws is a local nonprofit volunteer group dedicated to the care and shelter of our otherwise-neglected family pets. The services provided include rescue, medical resources, spay and neutering, and foster care. The foundation engages in animal care education and many animal interaction services in our Valley. A typical, if unfortunate, situation was in evidence with Executive Director Isabelle Gullo walking the Solvang streets with a friendly and beguiling Labradoodle named Cindy.

Cindy's people family had experienced a history of fights, with the husband becoming increasingly abusive and downright threatening in his drunken rages. A neighbor had called the sheriff, and the battered wife had been separated and sent to a hidden shelter home for protection. So much for the people, but the family dog was now in danger of harm with no wife left for the husband to beat on. The deputies took the dog under protection and called Paws, who immediately responded with shelter for the innocent family pet and the resources to find a foster home until the situation could be resolved.

The Labradoodle was on her way to a volunteer foster home that was known and used for this resource until the battered wife could find friendly housing and protection from a life of danger and then be safely reunited with Cindy. This was an extreme case, but not unusual, where Paws provides a humane service not found elsewhere.

Another typical service day in the life of Paws included a training session in our Solvang Fire Department facility. The firehouse day room was taken over by groupings of firefighters and Paws volunteers, demonstrating emergency care for animals that could be injured in traffic accidents or home fires. Fortunately for the attention span of the fire crews, the volunteer Paws staff were attractive young ladies who were doing the demonstration bandaging, splinting, and other rescue techniques. A number of tentative-looking dogs, who might have wanted to be elsewhere, were sprawled among the mentors and learners to pose as injured victims. The staff and firemen were earnestly bandaging and unwrapping, and even placing intravenous lines into the helpful dogs.

When the pandemic virus hit the community, the problems mounted like looming storm clouds. First the news and growing unease of the potential sickness, and then all the restrictions, from social distancing to home isolation, grew as the days of the coronavirus fight continued. Gradually, the economic fallout gripped the Valley as happened in all the world. Economic activity in the Valley became gradually nonexistent, and as businesses closed, many residents lost their jobs and livelihood. Local service organizations, public and private, stepped up to fill the needs of distressed families. Food banks and service organizations distributed food in many ways to families in need. The households were helped, but what of the family pets who also needed to eat?

Fortunately, Paws mobilized and devised ways to fill the gap of emergency food for the pets of families who had lost income and were in need for themselves and their pets. The organization's resources of volunteers, contributors, pet food suppliers, and connections with the agencies supplying family food were mobilized to secure and distribute food for pets. As of this writing, the sacks of people food left on needy doorsteps are being daily supplemented with sacks of dog and cat food, with the distribution carefully handled to avoid contamination. The households are grateful for food bank help, and the Valley animals are sustained by the good efforts of Paws.

The world and the Santa Ynez Valley, as yet, does not know how the pandemic will play out. How long and how severe the virus and the economic damage will be is still a matter of doubt and discussion. But we do know that, as in so many ways, the interaction of people and animals in the Valley is maintained in crisis. Animals and people share the Valley with mutual respect and sympathetic and fascinating interaction. And that is who we are. May it always be thus.

· 🐾 ·